Engaging North Korea:
The Role of Economic Statecraft

Policy Studies 59

Engaging North Korea:
The Role of Economic Statecraft

Stephan Haggard and Marcus Noland

Engaging North Korea: The Role of Economic Statecraft
Stephan Haggard and Marcus Noland

ISSN 1547-1349 (print) and 1547-1330 (electronic)
ISBN 978-1-932728-92-7 (print) and 978-1-932728-93-4 (electronic)

Hard copies of all titles, and free electronic copies of most titles, are available from:

East-West Center
1601 East-West Road
Honolulu, Hawai'i 96848-1601
Tel: 808.944.7111
EWCInfo@EastWestCenter.org
EastWestCenter.org/policystudies

In Asia, hard copies of all titles, and electronic copies of select Southeast Asia titles, co-published in Singapore, are available from:

Institute of Southeast Asian Studies
30 Heng Mui Keng Terrace
Pasir Panjang Road, Singapore 119614
publish@iseas.edu.sg
bookshop.iseas.edu.sg

Contents

List of Acronyms

ASEAN	Association of Southeast Asian Nations
BDA	Banco Delta Asia
CCP	Chinese Communist Party
COMTRADE	United Nations Commodity Trade Statistics Database
CRS	Congressional Research Service
CVID	complete, verifiable, irreversible dismantlement
DMZ	demilitarized zone
DOTS	Direction of Trade Statistics (IMF)
GDP	gross domestic product
HEU	highly enriched uranium
HFO	heavy fuel oil
HS	Harmonized System
IAEA	International Atomic Energy Agency
ICC	International Criminal Court
IFI	international financial institutions

IMF	International Monetary Fund
KEDO	Korean Peninsula Energy Development Organization
KINU	Korean Institute for National Unification
KITA	Korean International Trade Association
KOTRA	Korea Trade-Investment Promotion Agency
KPA	Korean People's Army
KWP	Workers' Party of Korea
LWR	light water reactors
NDC	National Defense Commission
NGO	nongovernmental organization
NLL	Northern Limit Line
NPT	Nuclear Non-Proliferation Treaty
PDS	public distribution system
PRC	People's Republic of China
PSI	Proliferation Security Initiative
SITC	Standard International Trade Classification
UN	United Nations
UNSC	United Nations Security Council
WMD	weapons of mass destruction

Executive Summary

Nowhere is the efficacy of economic inducements and sanctions more hotly contested than on the Korean peninsula. Assessments are sharply divided. Critics of engagement argue that positive inducements are fraught with moral hazard and the risk of blackmail, encouraging the very behavior they are designed to forestall. Proponents regard it as a strategy that has never consistently been put to the test.

This study makes three main points. The first has to do with domestic politics in North Korea, including both its capacity to absorb pressure and its interest in engagement. The extraordinary repressiveness of the regime clearly calls into question the utility of broad commercial sanctions against North Korea, assuming they could even be coordinated. There is some evidence that financial sanctions had an *economic* effect in both 2006 and again after 2009; by early 2011, the country was experiencing a steadily worsening food crisis and had pressed foreign capitals, the World Food Program, and nongovernmental organizations (NGOs) for assistance. Nonetheless, sanctions did not deter the regime from testing missiles and two nuclear devices, sinking the *Cheonan*, or shelling Yeonpyeong Island.

Evidence of North Korean intent to engage is elusive, but consistent with an interpretation that North Korean motivations varied over time. When the Bush administration came to office, North Korea was in a relatively reformist phase; this opening was almost completely missed by the Bush administration, which was preoccupied with intelligence on the country's highly enriched uranium (HEU) program. Over time, however, the mixed results of the reforms and the worsening external environment led to clear shifts in economic policy that are suggestive of deeper political changes in the regime. Particularly after 2005, and culminating with the disastrous currency reform of 2009, the regime's "military first" politics had taken a much harder form.

From August 2008, Kim Jong-il's likely stroke and the onset of the succession process frustrated prospects for engagement. These domestic political events coincided with a further "hardening" of the regime around core bases of support, a preoccupation with showing resolve, and a declining willingness to make tradeoffs. In combination, these domestic political shifts help explain the particularly unwelcoming stance North Korea took toward the incoming Obama administration, a stance that deeply colored Washington's reaction to the missile and nuclear tests of 2009.

A second finding is that the efforts of the Bush administration to pressure North Korea were consistently undermined by severe coordination problems. South Korea pursued a strategy of relatively unconditional engagement through 2007, and even Japan sought normalization until its policy was hijacked by domestic sensitivities over the earlier abductions of Japanese by North Koreans. But China's role was clearly pivotal. China has been consistent in its rhetorical commitment to denuclearization. Beijing has played a key role in brokering the talks, offered crucial inducements to keep the talks going, and even signaled its displeasure through support of multilateral statements and sanctions, particularly in 2009. Nevertheless, it has been consistently unwilling to use its vast economic influence to force a reckoning. To the contrary, North Korea's foreign economic relations have become more rather than less dependent on China, compounding the diplomatic difficulties of bringing pressure to bear on the country.

This conclusion gains force through a consideration of the North Korean response to pressure and sanctions. There is little evidence that ratcheting up pressure "worked"; to the contrary, it generated escalatory responses and poisoned negotiations. To the extent that it did work, it did so through a diplomatic process that spelled out for North Korea the benefits of complying with its international obligations, as well as the costs of not doing so. Sanctions can be justified on purely defensive grounds: as a means of limiting North Korea's weapons of mass destruction (WMD) or proliferation activity. But as a tactical tool to induce concessions at the bargaining table, the track record is mixed at best.

Yet the strategy of engagement and the use of inducements have encountered difficulties as well. Inducements have periodically worked to restart talks—for example, in the round of talks in 2005 that led to the September joint statement. There is also some limited evidence that very tightly calibrated reciprocal actions worked in 2008 before being politically derailed. But inducements "worked" only with respect to one component, albeit an important one, of the problem at hand: the production of fissile material at Yongbyon.

Addressing this issue effectively would have been a worthy achievement, and might have facilitated the so-called "third phase" of negotiations. It might also have forestalled the overt conflicts of 2009–10. But even if Yongbyon were disabled, a daunting agenda would have remained: an effective return to the Nuclear Non-Proliferation Treaty (NPT) and International Atomic Energy Agency (IAEA) inspections, proliferation, missiles, existing stockpiles of fissile material, and the weapons themselves. Compared to the production of plutonium, uranium enrichment would have posed particularly difficult inspection and verification issues, as subsequently learned from the stunning revelations of the extent of the country's HEU program in late 2010. Moreover, there was strong evidence that the North Koreans were unwilling to address important aspects of this remaining agenda, including proliferation and HEU in particular. With changing political dynamics in North Korea and the cushion provided by its external economic relations with China, such a bargaining process would have effectively acknowledged a nuclear North Korea for some time.

Thus, the story comes full circle: North Korea's political economy and its external relations render it remarkably insensitive to either sanctions or inducements. Instead, its behavior appears driven to a significant extent by domestic political considerations and the quest for regime survival. It is conceivable that as the regime consolidates power internally, it may be more willing to undertake risks and engage in negotiations more seriously and substantively. It is also possible that external constraints have simply not imposed enough pain, and that the country's worsening food shortages might push the regime to reengage or to exploit a humanitarian gesture.

The converse, however, appears at least equally plausible: that the post–Kim Jong-il leadership may be too politically insecure or divided to make meaningful concessions. The consolidation of power may only reinforce the preexisting trends toward a more hard-line and truculent policy. If so, the ultimate resolution of the North Korean nuclear issue may await fundamental change in the political regime.

Engaging North Korea:
The Role of Economic Statecraft

Introduction

Nowhere is the efficacy of economic inducements and sanctions more hotly contested than on the Korean peninsula. The signing of the Agreed Framework in 1994 successfully froze the operations of the Yongbyon nuclear complex but did not dismantle it.[1] Economic inducements, including the promise of light water reactors (LWR) and regular shipments of heavy fuel oil (HFO), were integral aspects of that deal. Engagement gained momentum following the election of Kim Dae-jung in December 1997 and the breakthrough of the North-South summit of June 2000.

From the outset, the Bush administration was much more skeptical of engagement than its predecessor. In November 2002, the administration chose to suspend HFO shipments in response to intelligence that North Korea had a clandestine uranium enrichment (HEU) program. North Korea interpreted this move as an abrogation of the Agreed Framework and escalated the crisis by withdrawing from the Nuclear Non-Proliferation Treaty (NPT) and, ultimately, announcing a nuclear capability in February 2005. The United States also escalated, in part by seeking to mobilize international pressure against North Korea and using new sanctions designed to limit the country's international financial transactions.

The Six Party Talks, initiated in 2003, became the diplomatic venue for addressing the nuclear crisis and, ultimately, yielded an important statement of principles in September 2005.[2] The statement of principles promised—albeit in vague terms—a package of economic inducements for North Korea. The talks quickly broke down following this agreement, in part because of the imposition of new financial sanctions by the United States against a Macao-based bank, Banco Delta Asia (BDA), which managed a number of North Korean accounts. North Korea once again escalated the crisis and tested a small nuclear device in October 2006.

Despite the test, the parties reached two important interim agreements in February and October 2007 that outlined a roadmap toward complete dismantlement of the Yongbyon facility. Again, economic inducements were an integral part of the bargain. The United States and North Korea reached an agreement with respect to the BDA accounts, and HFO shipments were promised in exchange for a step-by-step disabling of the reactor and other facilities.

Negotiations on the implementation of these agreements broke down at the end of the Bush administration in 2008 and, as of this writing (March 2011), have not been revived. Mutual recriminations over promised actions were at the core of the breakdown in 2008, with each side believing—with some reason—that the other had reneged.

President Barack Obama's statement of willingness to engage in his inaugural address was reciprocated by a new round of North Korean missile tests in April 2009 and a second nuclear test in May 2009. In March 2010, the North Koreans sank a South Korean naval vessel, the *Cheonan*, with the loss of 46 lives. In response to this string of provocations, the Obama administration pursued a two-track policy. The administration mobilized wide-ranging multilateral sanctions against North Korea and extended the financial sanctions initiated under the Bush administration. At the same time, however, it held out the olive branch of broadly worded and arguably vague inducements were Pyongyang to return to the talks. With the North Korean shelling of Yeonpyeong Island in November 2010, however, US and South Korean policy

> *The Obama administration mobilized multilateral sanctions against North Korea, yet held out an olive branch*

took a harder turn, downplaying the utility of talks and inducements and focusing on reestablishing the credibility of the alliance.

As can be seen from this brief narrative, the five parties[3] have tried a variety of economic incentives—both positive and negative—to dissuade North Korea from pursuing a nuclear option. Assessments of these efforts have been sharply divided. Critics of engagement share the conviction that positive inducements are fraught with moral hazard and the risk of blackmail, encouraging the very behavior they are designed to forestall (examples include Bolton 2007; Eberstadt 2004, 2009). Rather than engaging, the United States should lead the effort to place greater constraints on North Korea's foreign economic relations. Options for accomplishing this objective range from increased sanctions to more aggressive strategies of containment, such as interdiction of shipping, the enforcement of an embargo, or even military action.

The alternative narrative on engagement sees it as a strategy that has never consistently been put to the test, particularly by the United States.[4] The Clinton administration was politically constrained with respect to what it could offer North Korea, and faced difficulties even in meeting its obligations under the Agreed Framework (Hathaway and Tama 2004). Before suspicions had arisen about North Korea's HEU program, the Bush administration rejected the engagement approach of the late Clinton years, refused to negotiate with Pyongyang, and argued for a more muscular response to proliferation. The Bush administration eventually shifted to a policy of negotiating with North Korea, but deep divisions within the administration repeatedly undermined the credibility of these efforts and limited the material incentives it was willing to offer (see particularly Mazarr 2007).

Two progressive governments in South Korea, under Kim Dae-jung (1998–2004) and Roh Moo-hyun (2004–2009), actively sought to engage North Korea, and the Chinese have effectively committed to a strategy of deep engagement as well. These efforts appear to have yielded few concrete benefits, in part because they were swimming against the powerful current of US policy. If the decade-long effort to engage North Korea by the Kim and Roh governments appeared to yield little with respect to North Korea's nuclear posture, the more hawkish posture of the conservative Lee Myung-bak administration in South Korea has not done any better.

As these conflicting narratives suggest, North Korea has not only been impervious to nonproliferation efforts but to analytic consensus as well. Yet it cannot simultaneously be true that strategies of engagement are doomed to failure and that they could generate (or could have generated) denuclearization. A central—and perhaps insurmountable—methodological problem in seeking to resolve this debate is that the behavior predicted by the two models outlined above is often observationally equivalent; the behavior of an opportunist engaged in blackmail is indistinguishable from the likely response to an engagement strategy that is not deemed credible.

Nonetheless, this study seeks to untangle these contradictory assessments by considering three strands of evidence. In the first two sections, it examines two key structural constraints on the use of economic statecraft vis-à-vis North Korea. The first is the unusually closed and repressive nature of the regime and its base of political support in the party, security apparatus, and military. Although the regime did witness a reformist moment from 1998–2002, these signals were largely ignored by the Bush administration. As the crisis dragged on, the regime "hardened." Since 2005, the regime has embarked on a path of political and economic "reform in reverse." To the extent that economic reform signals a greater willingness to engage, the evidence from an analysis of domestic political and policy developments is hardly encouraging.

The second structural constraint on the use of both positive and negative inducements is the profound coordination problem among the five parties, especially among the United States, South Korea, and China. This coordination problem is not only a matter of the conflicting policy signals that result from differing diplomatic strategies toward North Korea, but is also exacerbated by the effects of sanctions on the structure of North Korea's foreign economic relations. As multilateral and bilateral sanctions mount, North Korea has become more integrated with countries that are willing to trade on an unconditional basis, most notably China. In addition, North Korea has sought out trading partners in the developing world, particularly in the Middle East, where proliferation concerns have become acute.

The third section provides an analytic narrative of the Six Party Talks through their collapse at the end of the Bush administration in 2008, and considers the evidence for the effects of inducements and constraints on progress in the talks. Sanctions generally induced defiance and escalation rather than cooperation, and appeared to weaken rather than strengthen moderate political forces, as Nincic (2005) has argued more generally. Highly targeted financial sanctions did appear to push the North Koreans back to the bargaining table, but to the extent that these sanctions "worked," they did so in conjunction with a partial lifting of sanctions, a resumption of negotiations, and the offer of new inducements.

However, the limited success of sanctions does not imply that positive inducements were successful, as this study will show through a reconstruction of the efforts to implement agreements reached in 2007 on the disablement of Yongbyon. In addition to the coordination problems noted above, both the negotiations and the implementation of agreements were plagued with profound credibility and sequencing problems. When inducements were extended in advance of compliance, they generated moral hazards: North Korea would simply pocket benefits and not reciprocate. Yet when inducements were offered only after compliance was complete—and particularly if such compliance involved irreversible actions, such as disabling or dismantling nuclear facilities—North Korea balked. These twin problems help account for the start-stop pattern of negotiations and their ultimate breakdown.

In the fourth section, this narrative is extended into the Obama administration, considering the new sanctions introduced in 2009 and the subsequent efforts to restart negotiations, both prior to and in the wake of the sinking of the *Cheonan*. The full litany of constraints on economic statecraft are once again visible, including both coordination problems and domestic political changes in North Korea that pushed policy in a more recalcitrant and uncooperative direction. But profound sequencing problems contributed to the deadlock as well, as the United States sought to channel negotiations through the Six Party Talks process to assure a continued focus on denuclearization, while North Korea expressed ambivalence about the Six Party process and sought out other venues, including bilateral negotiations with the United States.

Domestic Politics in North Korea: The Paradigmatic Hard Case

It has long been recognized that the effectiveness of sanctions will depend on political characteristics of the target state (for example, Pape 1997; Brooks 2002). In recent years, several efforts have been made to extend these observations to the analysis of the political economy of inducements as well (see particularly Drezner 1999–2000; Kahler and Kastner 2006; Solingen 1994, 2007). Both regime type and the composition of political support coalitions have been invoked as relevant factors in this regard, and on both counts, North Korea provides a particularly difficult target for economic statecraft.

The effectiveness of sanctions will depend in the first instance on the political capacity of the target state to absorb economic shocks. If leaders do not face significant domestic audience costs, sanctions will only bite if targeted either on the political elite itself or on politically significant constituencies (Cortright and Lopez 2002, Brooks 2002). However, it is not adequately appreciated that authoritarian regimes are also likely to be less sensitive to the political benefits of many economic inducements (Brooks 2002, Kahler and Kastner 2006). This expectation stems in part from the fact that autocratic rulers are not as responsive to the welfare of the median citizen as are democratic ones.[5] Inducements are more likely to be attractive to authoritarian regimes when they provide material benefits to the leadership or fungible resources over which the regime has direct control, conditions that are not likely to be politically appealing for the country deploying them.

Authoritarian regimes are less sensitive to sanctions than democracies, but may also be less interested in inducements

As Solingen (2007) has argued most persuasively, the responsiveness of governments to external incentives also stems from the composition of political coalitions. Authoritarian regimes based on inward-looking coalitions are likely to be indifferent to both sanctions and certain types of inducements. The mechanism through which these instruments of economic statecraft purportedly work is through the costs they impose or benefits they provide to firms or other actors in the foreign sector broadly conceived, i.e., those engaged in—or who could benefit from—foreign trade, investment, or aid. These costs and benefits, in turn, induce political leaders to adjust foreign policy in a more cooperative direction.

But in regimes rooted in inward-oriented political coalitions, these processes are unlikely to operate. Key bases of political support either are indifferent to economic constraints and inducements or prefer to retain the uncooperative foreign policies, including weapons programs, that such incentives are designed to mitigate. Increased economic openness may even pose risks for regimes rooted in inward-looking coalitions—for example, by threatening existing rents or through increased information flows.

Turning to the evidence on these two lines of argument—on regime type and coalitions—it is useful to first restate the obvious: the North Korean regime is unusually repressive by any standard, and its capacity to impose costs on its population is extraordinary.[6]

This can be seen most clearly in the economic collapse and famine of the mid-1990s. The dissolution of the Soviet Union and the subsequent Russian demand for hard currency payment for needed inputs resulted in a slow-moving collapse of the industrial economy in the first half of the 1990s. Deprived of needed inputs, particularly fertilizer and fuel for irrigation, agricultural output also went into a secular decline, forcing a draconian compression of rations delivered through the public distribution system (PDS).

In part because of the first nuclear crisis (1992–94), it was not until the spring of 1995 that the regime appealed for external assistance. Aid was rapidly forthcoming, but by the time of this appeal the famine was raging. Estimates vary widely, but the famine probably killed between 600,000 and 1 million people, or roughly 3 to 5 percent of the pre-crisis population (Goodkind and West 2001, Lee 2003, Haggard and Noland 2007). Even Pyongyang and the lower levels of the military and party were probably not spared from the tribulations of this so-called "arduous march" period.

How the regime managed to survive this shock is an intriguing tale in its own right, but one reason is that Kim Jong-il had established personal control of the state apparatus and an effective base of support in the party, military, and security apparatus well prior to his father's death in 1994 (McEachern 2008, Lim 2009, Haggard and Pinkston 2010). In short, the survival of the regime was due in part to the very factors likely to make it immune to economic statecraft. Despite a well-managed succession process, Kim Jong-il openly turned toward the military following his assumption of the country's leadership. He even went so far as to initiate an ideological innovation—the so-called "military first politics" or "*songun*"—a pretty unambiguous statement of the regime's core base of political support.[7] The constitutional revision of September 1998 further strengthened the power of the National Defense Commission (NDC) and its chairman.[8]

Table 1 outlines the membership of the NDC at two points in time (2003 and 2009) and is suggestive of the regime's dependence on the military, the security apparatus, and the military industrial complex. Clearly, these political forces are inclined to prioritize national defense over other objectives, including economic reform, and are less likely to be accommodative with respect to measures seen as diluting the country's military capabilities.

The September 2010 Workers' Party of Korea (KWP) conference did not formally pass power from Kim Jong-il to his son; Kim Jong-il maintained all top party positions, as well as military and government positions. Nonetheless, the conference clearly served as a coming-out party for heir apparent Kim Jong-un. A central theme of the conference was the continued role of personalism and family connections. Prior to the convening of the conference, Kim Jong-un and Kim Jong-il's sister, Kim Kyong-hui, were promoted to the rank of four-star general despite no known military background or even training. Kim Jong-un became vice chairman of the Central Military Commission, as well as a member of the Central Committee (but not the politburo). Kim Kyong-hui became a member of the politburo, and her husband, Jang Song-thaek, was made an alternate. But the apparent strengthening of the party should not necessarily be interpreted as a weakening of military influence; to the contrary, the conference provided further evidence of the interpenetration of the military and the party at the highest levels. Of the five positions in the presidium, in addition to Kim Jong-il's chairmanship of the KWP, two were military (although one of these two officeholders, Marshal Jo Myong-rok, subsequently died). In the official photograph of the delegates, newly promoted Vice Marshall Ri Yong-ho, the other military appointment to the presidium, is front and center, seated directly to Kim Jong-il's right, between the elder and younger Kims.

At first blush, these recent political developments would appear to signal strong continuity and a virtual textbook example of Solingen's inward-looking coalition: a rigidly authoritarian state socialist economy coupled with a highly personalist leadership relying on the party,

Table 1. Membership of the National Defense Commission 2003 and 2009		
	National Defense Commission of the 11th Supreme People's Assembly (September 2003)	**National Defense Commission of the 12th Supreme People's Assembly (April 2009)**
Chairman	**Kim Jong-il** KWP Secretary General and Supreme Commander	**Kim Jong-il** KWP Secretary General and Supreme Commander

Deputy Chairman	• **Yon Hyong-muk**
	  Chief Secretary, Jakang Province
	• **Lee Yong-mu**
	  Vice Marshal
		• **Kim Young-chun**
		  Minister of People's Armed Forces
		• **Lee Yong-mu**
		  Vice Marshal
		• **Oh Kuk-ryul**
		  Director of Operations Department, KWP

Members	• **Kim Young-chun**
	  Chief of General Staff, KPA
	• **Chun Byung-ho**
	  Minister of Military Industry, KWP
	• **Kim Il-chu**
	  Minister of People's Armed Forces
	• **Paik Se-bong**
	  Chairman of the Second Economy
	• **Choi Yong-su**
	  Minister of People's Security
		• **Chun Byung-ho**
		  Minister of Military Industry, KWP
		• **Kim Il-chu**
		  First Vice Minister of People's Armed Forces
		• **Paik Se-bong**
		  Chairman of the Second Economy
		• **Chang Sung-taek**
		  Minister of Administration, KWP
		• **Choo Sang-sung**
		  Minister of People's Security
		• **Woo Dong-cuk**
		  First Vice Minister of National Security Agency
		• **Choo Kyu-chang**
		  First Vice Minister of Military Industry, KWP
		• **Kim Jong-kak**
		  First Vice Director General of Political Affairs

Source: Choi 2009

military, and security apparatus. However, a closer analysis of developments suggests that a period of political consolidation and crisis management in the immediate aftermath of Kim Il-sung's death (1994–1997) was followed by a brief period of cautious economic reform in the 1998–2002 period, before a combination of factors pushed the regime in an anti-reformist direction in the mid-2000s.

> *The famine prompted a period of economic reform before anti-reformist forces became ascendant in the mid-2000s*

Evidence of this brief reformist moment can be found in several developments during this period (Frank 2005). First, the new constitution itself included cautious reforms, including constitutional provisions that granted greater scope for private activity (Article 24), for incentives within the state sector (Article 33), and for foreign trade and investment (Articles 36 and 37). But they were also reflected in major institutional changes, including the restoration of the cabinet to a more "normal" role with more substantial authority over economic management (particularly Article 119). As Carlin and Wit (2006) show in their careful review of North Korean economic publications, this period witnessed a surprisingly open debate over economic strategy, focusing on the weight that should be given to heavy industry, and even the military industrial complex, as opposed to light industry and agriculture.

Evidence of this shift can also be found in Kim Jong-il's "on-the-spot guidance" tours of different work units in the country, a commonly used indicator of contemporary policy priorities (Figure 1). With the exception of an extraordinary emphasis on economic units during the peak famine period of 1996, the years from 1990 to 1997 witnessed a steady increase in visits to military units. In 1998, however, visits to economic sites start to increase in share. From the onset of the nuclear crisis through 2007, the military was once again the favored destination. Although visits to economic units increased after that, in context they represent a reversion to a more rigidly state socialist development path.

It is beyond the scope of this essay to trace the subsequent course of reform in detail, but its timing is crucial for understanding the political economy of the country's foreign policy. In the aftermath of the famine, the regime was constrained to undertake incremental and ad hoc

Figure 1. Appearances by Kim Jong-il, 1990–2010

percent

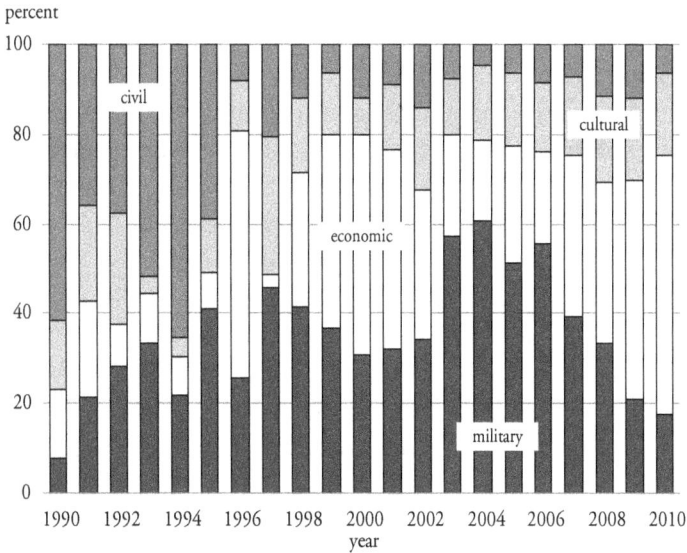

Sources: North Korea's Korean Central News Agency (KCNA) and Korean Central Television (KCTV).

reforms, but in 2002, the government launched a major set of policy changes. There are ample grounds for criticizing the economic policy changes as a limited and flawed effort, but they ratified the controlled growth of markets, reset prices, and began or continued incremental reforms of the cooperatives and state-owned enterprises.

With the benefit of hindsight, however, these shifts may have constituted not only a change in economic policy, but a more fundamental strategic reorientation built around three components: a revitalized military deterrent, a partial demobilization of conventional forces, and economic policy changes (Noland 2004, Frank 2005). The deterrent would have rested on the ongoing development of the country's missile capabilities, which would offset the long-run decline in other conventional forces. As subsequently seen, it was the United States and other regional powers that responded strongly to the open pursuit of even a minimal nuclear deterrent. But North Korea's dalliance with a nuclear capability could be seen as a hedging strategy against the risk associated with deteriorating conventional capabilities.

With an adequate missile deterrent, the regime could have contemplated a partial demobilization of its forward-deployed ground forces.

This move would not only have reduced the drain of military spending, but also provided the basis for North-South détente and weakened the justification for a large US force presence, an ongoing strategic objective.

Economic reform would play a number of important roles in this strategic reorientation, most obviously in reversing the economic decline, of which the famine was the most obvious manifestation. Economic reform would have permitted a rebuilding of the state sector, while simultaneously employing demobilized troops.

Reform also had a clear foreign policy component. Diplomatic initiatives during this period suggested a renewed willingness to engage the outside world. North Korea reengaged with China following a period of some tension and held summits with South Korea (June 2000), Russia (August 2001), and Japan (September 2002). These diplomatic openings had important economic components, largely in the form of promises of aid, as well as expanded commercial relations. These included not only the opening of the South Korean aid spigot and the deepening of economic ties with China, but also the promise of a substantial post-colonial claims payment from Japan as part of diplomatic normalization with that country.

Yet the timing of the reform proved highly inauspicious. Within months of launching the 2002 reforms, the second nuclear crisis had broken. The October revelation of a uranium enrichment (HEU) program, and the revelation that North Korea had indeed abducted Japanese citizens, made this gambit diplomatically unsustainable. As a result, the regime was left with the problematic legacy of the partial economic reforms of July 2002, but without the complementary political and economic payoffs that were required to make the reforms work. The internal debate over the merits of reform continued through 2005 (Carlin and Wit 2006), but, thereafter, signs began to accumulate that hard-liners were winning the policy battles and reforms were being reversed, with highly adverse economic effects.

An early indication of this new direction was the decision in August 2005 to reinstate the public distribution system (PDS) and to ban private trading in grain. The post-reform effort to re-assert state control was not limited to the food economy, but included a wider assault on market activity and the cross-border trade.[9] The latter posed particular challenges to the North Korean leadership because it jeopardized the government's monopoly on information about the outside world. The reactionary tenor of government policy was vividly represented by a revival of the 1950s Stalinist "Chollima" movement of Stakhanovite exhortation and the initiation of "speed-battle" mobilization campaigns, but these changes were not just temporary or ad hoc. In 2009, revisions to the planning law overturned reforms introduced in 2001 and 2002, codifying a more top-down planning process (Institute for Far Eastern Studies 2010a).

The culmination of the anti-reform drive came on November 30, 2009, with the introduction of a surprise confiscatory currency reform aimed at crushing market activity and reviving orthodox socialism (Haggard and Noland 2010a). The move had a chilling effect on virtually all economic activity, both public and private, and ushered in a period of acute shortages and enormous rise in prices, most importantly of food. The government was ultimately forced to accommodate itself to economic realities by reopening previously banned markets and allowing the use of foreign currency. The government also sought to revive and deepen the China trade. But whether these adjustments serve as a springboard for more wide-ranging reform or are only a tactical adjustment in the face of pressing economic constraints and food shortages remains to be seen.[10]

This brief overview of domestic economic and political developments is designed to make several simple points. First, the capacity of the regime to absorb the adverse effects of sanctions is extraordinarily high. A regime capable of surviving a famine that killed up to a million people is not likely to be swayed by sanctions threatening marginal changes in trade and investment flows. Moreover, the regime has shown the capacity to make short-run tactical adjustments—such as allowing markets to function or seeking external support—that have at least partly offset the most extreme deprivation. Sanctions would have to be extraordinarily focused and "smart" to have effect, and, for reasons explored in the next section, such actions are difficult—although not impossible—to achieve.

> *A regime capable of surviving a famine that killed up to a million people is not likely to be swayed by limited sanctions*

Second, the political basis of the regime appears to conform quite closely to Solingen's model of an inward-looking coalition that is likely to be relatively indifferent to both economic constraints and inducements. However, this assessment overlooks important shades of gray. Political and policy developments in the immediate post-1998 period suggest a brief effort to combine "military first" politics with a mild reformism. But as shown in more detail below, the opening provided by these events was completely missed by the Bush administration. With the onset of the crisis and accumulating problems in the reforms themselves, the political base of the regime shifted. The value of economic inducements, particularly highly general ones such as the lifting of sanctions, appeared less attractive than inducements that the political elite could control or tax more directly: transfers of food and fuel, fees (such as those made in connection with the operations of the Kaesong Industrial Complex), or straight cash payments (such as those that were subsequently found to have funded the 2000 North-South summit). More importantly, the cost-benefit calculation with respect to the pursuit of nuclear weapons also shifted, making it harder to secure cooperation using either inducements or constraints. This was particularly the case given the coordination problems facing the five parties.

The Coordination Problem: North Korea's Foreign Economic Relations

As has long been noted in the sanctions literature, the effectiveness of sanctions is contingent on cooperation among the target state's trading partners (for example, Hufbauer, Schott, and Elliott 2009; Elliott 2010). Throughout the course of the crisis, those parties seeking to pressure North Korea, particularly the United States, found themselves in conflict with those who were willing to engage with it, most importantly China and South Korea.

However, evidence points to coordination problems in a more dynamic sense as well. Over time, North Korea has gravitated toward those trading partners that place the least restrictions on trade and investment, making it increasingly difficult to impose effective sanctions.

This section outlines the material foundations of this coordination problem by considering the evolution of North Korea's foreign economic relations. The following sections consider the political dimensions of the coordination problem. They trace both the difficulty the United States had in mobilizing pressure on North Korea, but also the difficulty that South Korea and China had in seeking to engage it.

North Korea's Changing Foreign Economic Relations

North Korea does not provide data on its own trade, meaning that it must be constructed from trading partners (see Haggard and Noland 2008 and Appendix 1 for a more detailed discussion of these issues). This data is vulnerable to significant discrepancies, but with the appropriate caveats in mind, several estimates of the direction of North Korea's trade with select partners are presented. Figure 2 includes data taken directly from the Korea Trade-Investment Promotion Agency (KOTRA) and shows North Korea's total trade with the five interlocutors in the Six Party Talks—the United States, China, Japan, South Korea, and Russia—for 2000 through 2008 ("total trade").

KOTRA has a reasonable track record in eliminating obvious discrepancies, and this data has the advantage of constituting a consistent series for the entire period of the crisis from a single source. However, compared to data produced by the United Nations (UN) and the

Figure 2. Shares of North Korea's Total Trade (KOTRA) and Imports (Haggard and Noland)

percent of North Korean total trade and imports

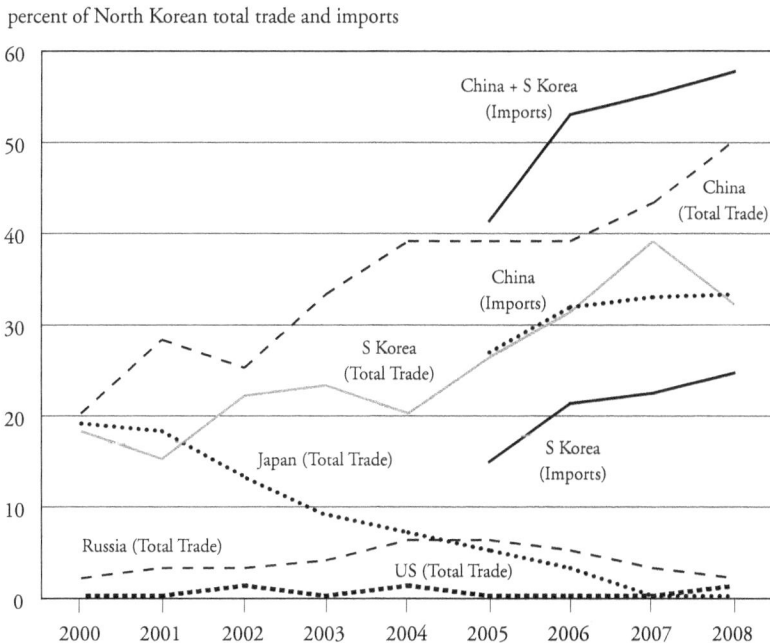

Source: KOTRA (Korea Trade-Investment Promotion Agency), http://www.kotra.go.kr.

International Monetary Fund (IMF), the KOTRA data significantly underestimates the growth of North Korea's trade with many countries, particularly in the developing world. We, therefore, provide an alternative estimate of the significance of North Korean imports from China and South Korea for the period 2004–2007, based on different estimates of North Korea's total imports (Figure 2, "imports"; see Haggard and Noland 2010b). The KOTRA estimates might be viewed as the high-end of the likely range for these two important trading partners, with our estimates more likely to represent the lower end.

The first point to note is that China and South Korea alone probably account for 55 percent to 80 percent of North Korea's trade, a wide range but one that is obviously of great significance. Second, whatever the *level* of trade with China and South Korea, their share has clearly increased since the onset of the crisis. The third point is that despite the high partner concentration of North Korea's trade, its vulnerability to sanctions has not necessarily increased. Those countries more inclined to sanction North Korea—the United States and Japan—have negligible economic exchange with the country. After the sinking of the *Cheonan*, South Korean trade with the North outside of the Kaesong Industrial Complex also ground to a halt, thus further increasing China's share. Although the United States has devised new financial sanctions against North Korea, there is little room among these "high sanctions" countries to wield influence by further curtailing commercial trade outside of a decision to close Kaesong. At this point, trade can only be used as an inducement in the form of the promise to lift sanctions.

While trade with countries disposed to sanctions has fallen, North Korea's trade has shifted toward countries that have proven unwilling to use their leverage for nonproliferation ends. This adjustment process was not without cost; North Korea paid for the loss of trade and remittances from Japan, as well as the end of aid, and later trade, with South Korea.

> **Reduced trade with Japan and South Korea was rerouted through willing intermediaries in China**

But these costs should not be exaggerated, and there is no doubt some leakage as trade with both Japan and South Korea is partly "rerouted" through willing intermediaries in China.

Figure 3. North Korean Trade with the World vs. the Middle East, 2000–2008

Index, 2000=100

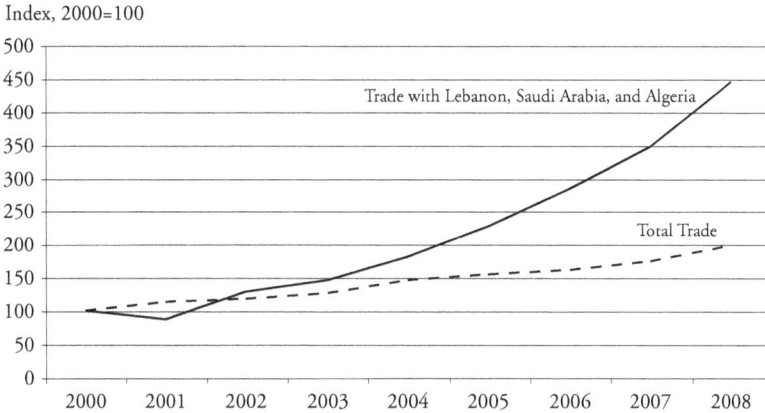

Sources: KOTRA, IMF DOT (Direction of Trade Statistics).

This coordination problem becomes even more apparent if possible measurement problems with the KOTRA data are considered. In recent years, developing countries such as Brazil, Thailand, and India have increased their trade with North Korea; in 2007, according to the UN/IMF data, these three countries accounted for more than 10 percent of both North Korean imports and exports. Even more revealing are developments with the Middle East. Figure 3 aggregates trade with three countries—Algeria, Saudi Arabia, and Lebanon—that report non-negligible trade with North Korea on a consistent basis and shows an index of their trade growth compared to the growth of total trade. The index almost certainly understates the true growth of trade between North Korea and the region, given underreporting and illicit trade. And it does not capture foreign direct investment, particularly from the Egyptian conglomerate Orascom (Noland 2009a). Nonetheless, the index shows a dramatic increase in relations with these three countries when compared to the growth of overall trade.

The China Trade

A closer look at China–North Korea and North-South trade provides further insights into the political dynamics of these two critical bilateral relationships. Figure 4 provides a long-run overview of the trade

Figure 4. China–North Korea Trade, 1982–2009

USD, Billions

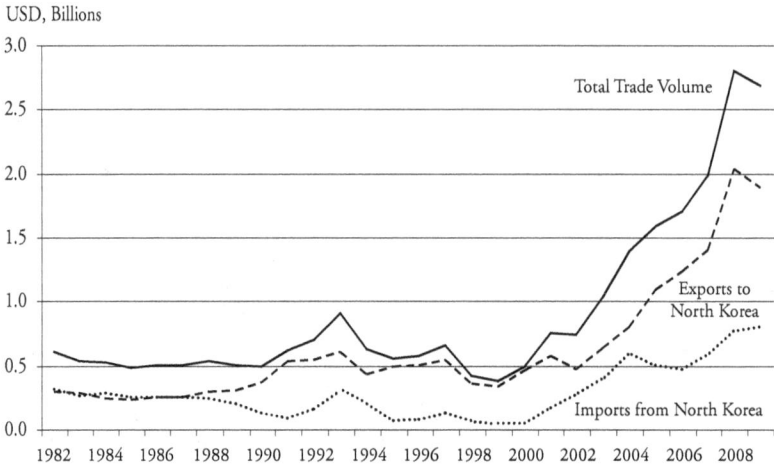

Source: Ministry of Commerce of the People's Republic of China.

relationship with China from 1982 through 2009. China stepped into the breach as trade with Russia collapsed in the early 1990s. Trade generally remained at relatively low and constant levels until the political thaw and tentative reforms of the post-1998 period. The subsequent explosion in trade clearly overlaps with the onset of the second nuclear crisis.

A second noteworthy feature of this bilateral relationship is the emergence of quite large deficits. These deficits were financed in part by surpluses with South Korea, but, nonetheless, almost certainly imply corresponding financial inflows in the form of aid, the continuation of "friendship prices," the accumulation of arrears, and foreign direct investment.

A third feature of the bilateral relationship is its increasingly commercial nature. China–North Korea trade ranges from aid (on which no data is publicly available) to purely commercial border trade with the Korean Chinese community in the Chinese border provinces. Between these two ideal types—aid and the market—lies a very wide gray area of trade with state-owned and private companies, including foreign ones. Both limited data, including survey data collected on Chinese enterprises doing business in North Korea, and anecdotal evidence suggest that the dramatic expansion of bilateral trade ties is undoubtedly coming from the growth of the purely commercial and quasi-commercial shares.

There is one positive byproduct of the deepening China–North Korea tie: it is increasing the availability of an array of communications and foreign-origin cultural products that directly undermine the government's monopoly on information. These range from small televisions capable of receiving Chinese broadcasts in border areas to South Korean videos and DVDs, and even mobile phones. Although the government is actively seeking to quash these developments, it is difficult to both allow integration with China to grow

> *The increase in trade with China undermines North Korea's monopoly on information*

and to fully control this important incidental effect. Consumption of foreign news and entertainment products is rising and, according to refugee surveys, is associated with more critical views of the regime (Haggard and Noland, 2011, forthcoming).

On balance, however, the general unwillingness of the Chinese to use economic instruments to pressure North Korea[11], the observed growth in bilateral trade and investment, and the increasingly commercial nature of China–North Korea trade all cast doubt on the likely effectiveness of commercial sanctions. A visual inspection of the data in Figure 4 certainly suggests that sanctions have not had any material impact on China's trade with North Korea, but the proposition can be tested by modeling the effects of the two major multilateral sanctions efforts on China–North Korea trade: those imposed in the wake of the 2006 nuclear test (UN Security Council Resolution 1718, October 14, 2006) and the 2009 nuclear test (UN Security Council Resolution 1784, June 12, 2009).[12]

These sanctions did not directly impinge on purely commercial trade, in part because of Chinese reluctance to support more wide-ranging commercial sanctions.[13] It goes without saying that South Korea does not export weapons to North Korea, and, in recent years, China has not reported the export of heavy arms either.[14] Luxury goods are a different story, however. China's report to the United Nations Security Council (UNSC) sanctions committee does not even mention sanctioned luxury goods pursuant to UNSC Resolution 1718

Stephan Haggard and Marcus Noland

(Congressional Research Service 2010), but a number of other countries did publish detailed lists. As shown in Table 2, these lists exhibit considerable consistency across countries.

In the absence of a Chinese list of sanctioned luxury goods, Figure 5 reports Chinese exports of luxury goods to North Korea defined in three ways. The first variant ("Australian list—SITC") takes the Australian list in Table 2 and maps the verbal description of the sanctioned luxury products to Standard International Trade Classification (SITC) categories. The second variant ("Japanese list") is based on KOTRA (2006), which attempted to map the Japanese sanctions list to detailed product categories using the Harmonized System (HS) (Kim 2006). The third variant ("Australian list—HS") reconstructs the Australian list using KOTRA's HS codes, which tend to be more narrowly drawn than the Australian SITC list. As can be seen in Figure 5, Chinese exports of luxury goods to North Korea did not fall to zero in 2007 under any variant; indeed, luxury goods exports increased between 2006 and 2007 under all three definitions.[15] Resolution 1718 appears to have had no impact on Chinese behavior.

But the two resolutions, and particularly 1874, contain a number of provisions that might disrupt North Korea's commercial relations, including a request to both international institutions and member states that they not extend to North Korea new grants, financial assistance, or concessional loans, and that they exhibit "vigilance" with respect to

Figure 5. Chinese Luxury Goods Exports to North Korea

USD, Millions

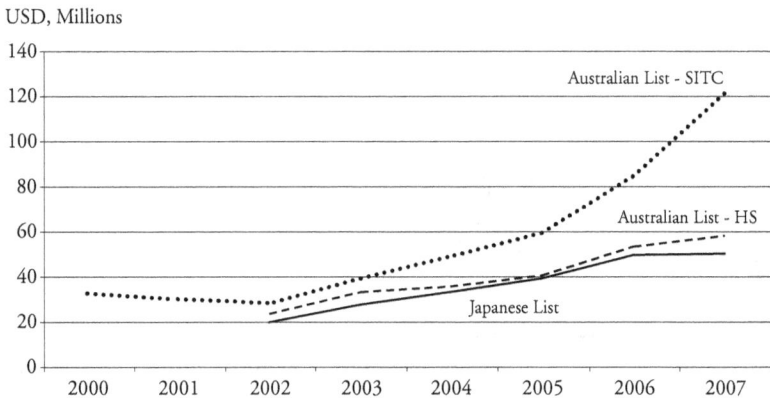

Sources: UN COMTRADE, KOTRA (2006).

	USA	EU	Australia	Canada	Japan
Food Items		Caviar and caviar substitutes Truffles and preparations thereof	Caviar Crustaceans (all), e.g., rock lobsters Abalone Molluscs and aquatic inver-tebrates, e.g., oyster in any form	Gourmet foods and ingredients Lobster	Caviar and caviar substitutes prepared from fish eggs Meat of bovine animals, frozen (beef) Fish fillets, frozen (tuna)
Tobacco	Tobacco and tobacco products	High-quality cigars and cigarillos	Tobacco products	Cigarettes	Tobacco
Beverages	Alcoholic beverages: wine, beer, ales, and liquor	High-quality wines (including sparkling wines), spirits, and spirituous beverages	Wine and spirits (all kinds)	Alcoholic beverages	Alcoholic beverages
Cosmetics	Perfumes and toilet waters Cosmetics, including beauty and makeup products	Luxury per-fumes, toilet waters, and cosmetics, in-cluding beauty and makeup products	Perfumes and toilet waters Cosmetics (all)	Perfumes	Perfumes and toilet waters Cosmetics (beauty and makeup products)
Apparel	Apparel: leather articles Apparel: silk articles Designer cloth-ing: leather ap-parel and clothing accessories	High-quality garments, cloth-ing accessories, and shoes (regardless of their material)		Designer clothing	
Fur	Fur skins and artificial furs		Furs	Furs	Fur skins and artificial fur products

Table 2. Luxury Goods Ban Lists

Table 2. Luxury Goods Ban Lists (continued)

	USA	EU	Australia	Canada	Japan
Fashion Accessories	Leather travel goods, vanity cases, binocular and camera cases, handbags, wallets, silk scarves		Leather travel goods, apparel, and clothing accessories	Clothing accessories	Leather bags, clothes, and others
Transportation	Luxury automobiles (and motor vehicles): automobiles and other motor vehicles to transport people (other than public transport), including station wagons Racing cars, snowmobiles, and motorcycles Personal transportation devices (stand-up motorized scooters)	Luxury vehicles for the transport of persons on earth, air, or sea, as well as their accessories and spare parts	Automobiles and other vehicles to transport people		Motorcars Motorcycles
Aquatic Vehicles	Yachts and other aquatic recreational vehicles (such as personal watercraft)		Yachts and pleasure craft		Motorboats, yachts, and others
Flooring	Rugs and tapestries	Hand-knotted carpets, hand-woven rugs, and tapestries	Carpets		Carpets and other textile floor coverings
Jewelry	Jewelry with pearls, gems, precious and semi-precious stones (including diamonds, sapphires, rubies, and emeralds) Jewelry of precious metal or of metal clad with precious metal	Pearls, precious and semi-precious stones, articles of pearls, jewelry, gold- or silver-smith articles Cutlery of precious metal or plated or clad with precious metal	Jewelry Precious and semi-precious stones (including diamonds and pearls) Silver and gold precious metals	Jewelry Gems Precious metals	Jewelry Natural or cultured pearls, precious or semi-precious stones Precious metals and metal work

Table 2. Luxury Goods Ban Lists (continued)				
	USA	**EU**	**Australia**	**Canada**	**Japan**
Electronic Items	Flat-screen, plasma, or LCD panel televisions or other video monitors or receivers (including highdefinition televisions), and any television larger than 29 inches; DVD players Personal digital assistants (PDAs) Personal digital music players Computer laptops	High-end electronic items for domestic use	Consumer electronics (televisions, videos, DVD players, PDAs, laptops, MP3 players, and any other relevant exports)	Televisions Computers Other electronic devices	Televisions Portable digital automatic data processing machines
Photographic Equipment		High-end electrical/electronic or optical apparatus for recording and reproducing sound and images	Photographic equipment		Cinematographic cameras and projectors Apparatus for recording and reproducing sound and images
Watches/ Clocks	Luxury watches: wrist, pocket, and others with a case of precious metal or of metal clad with precious metal	Luxury clocks and watches and their parts	Watches and clocks	Watches	Wrist watches and other watches
Works of Art	Works of art (including paintings, original sculptures, and statuary), antiques (more than 100 years old) Collectible items, including rare coins and stamps	Works of art, collectors' pieces, and antiques Coins and banknotes, not being legal tender	Works of art (all)		Works of art, collectors' pieces, and antiques

	USA	EU	Australia	Canada	Japan
Table 2. Luxury Goods Ban Lists (continued)					
Musical Instru- ments	Musical instruments	High-quality musical instruments			Musical instruments; parts and accessories of such articles
Sports Equip- ment	Recreational sports equipment	Articles and equipment for skiing, golfing, diving, and water sports	Sports equipment	Sporting goods	
Fountain Pens	Fountain pens		Fountain pens		Fountain pens
Drinking Glass	Items of lead crystal	High-quality lead crystal glassware	Drinking glasses (lead crystal)		Drinking glasses (lead crystal)
Others	Tableware of porcelain or bone china	High-quality tableware of porcelain, chi- na, stone- or earthenware, or fine pottery Purebred horses Articles and equipment for billiard, auto- matic bowling, casino games, and games ope- rated by coins or banknotes	Electronic entertainment/ software	Private aircraft	

Source: Noland 2009b

existing aid programs. The resolution also calls on member states to inspect all cargo on their territory believed to contain prohibited items, and authorizes members to inspect vessels on the high seas or to escort them to port if there are reasonable grounds to believe that they are carrying prohibited cargo.[16]

Moreover, sanctions might be expected to have effects beyond trade in proscribed products. China may choose to implement sanctions measures quietly rather than to openly align with the United States and Japan on the issue. If this were the case, the tests and sanctions might have a greater effect than their limited product scope would lead one to believe. Second, the missile and nuclear tests and the subsequent sanctions might affect private commercial behavior. The increase in political tensions might drive up the risk premium on all trade and financial transactions with North Korea and, thus, discourage them at the margin.

To test for these broader effects of the two nuclear tests and sanctions episodes, this study specified some simple econometric models of Chinese exports to North Korea, using quarterly data from the third quarter of 2001 through the second quarter of 2010 (Table 3; see Noland 2009b and Appendix 2 for a more detailed explanation of the data and models). The models include a time trend, seasonal dummies, an indicator of aggregate demand in North Korea (real gross domestic product, GDP, which, when included, eliminated the significance of the time trend), and the inverse of the black market exchange rate (to capture the North Korean price level). The effects of the tests and sanctions were captured with dummies for all post-test and sanctions quarters (i.e., a dummy from the fourth quarter of 2006 and a second from the third quarter of 2009). The coefficient on the 2009 sanctions dummy can be interpreted as the effect of the second test and sanctions conditional on the existence of the first. The models were estimated on total Chinese exports to North Korea, and also on exports of food, fuel, and food and fuel combined. The models of food and fuel were designed to test for the possibility that China might be quietly manipulating its aid to North Korea; these two product categories are widely believed to be those for which the Chinese maintain at least some subsidy to the North.

The results of the models are striking, and confirm what one would already suspect from a consideration of the rapid growth in trade visible in Figure 4. In the model of total Chinese exports, the coefficients on the two sanctions dummies are actually positive and significant; far from reducing total exports to North Korea in the aftermath of the two tests, China actually increased them. In the models of price-adjusted exports of food, fuel, and food and

China has actually increased trade with North Korea since the onset of the nuclear crisis

Table 3. China–North Korea Trade

	Log total Chinese exports to North Korea			Log Chinese cereal exports to North Korea	Log Chinese fuel exports to North Korea	Log Chinese cereal & fuel exports to North Korea
	(3.1)	(3.2)	(3.3)	(3.4)	(3.5)	(3.6)
Log North Korean real GDP index	36.382***	34.591***	34.015***	-29.193	-0.245	-1.284
	(5.830)	(4.427)	(2.695)	(45.855)	(12.662)	(12.201)
(price proxy) log inverse exchange rate index	-0.011	0.019		0.514	-0.050	0.104
	(0.132)	(0.115)		(1.148)	(0.329)	(0.317)
2006 sanction dummy	1.149***	1.113***	1.109***	-0.332	0.448	0.350
	(0.196)	(0.179)	(0.174)	(1.913)	(0.512)	(0.494)
2009 sanction dummy	0.664**	0.692**	0.660***	4.507	0.154	0.588
	(0.313)	(0.303)	(0.228)	(3.139)	(0.867)	(0.836)
Logged time trend	-0.123					
	(0.255)					
q_2	1.245***	1.241***	1.241***		1.731***	1.290**
	(0.190)	(0.187)	(0.184)		(0.536)	(0.516)
q_3	1.089***	1.087***	1.096***		1.044*	0.730
	(0.198)	(0.195)	(0.185)		(0.559)	(0.538)
q_4	1.211***	1.204***	1.213***		1.529**	1.173**
	(0.197)	(0.194)	(0.184)		(0.555)	(0.534)

Table 3. China–North Korea Trade (continued)

	Log total Chinese exports to North Korea			Log Chinese cereal exports to North Korea	Log Chinese fuel exports to North Korea	Log Chinese cereal & fuel exports to North Korea
	(3.1)	(3.2)	(3.3)	(3.4)	(3.5)	(3.6)
Constant	-117.253***	-109.200***	-106.462***	178.295	48.230	53.898
	(27.015)	(20.919)	(12.620)	(216.790)	(59.838)	(57.661)
Observations	36	36	36	36	36	36
R-squared	0.954	0.953	0.953	0.142	0.346	0.249
p value	0	0	0	0.298	0.074	0.274
log likelihood	-13.16	-13.31	-13.33	-100.5	-51.15	-49.81
Durbin Watson d-statistic	2.266	2.206	2.216	1.960	1.639	1.734
Durbin's alternative test for autocorrelation, Prob>chi2	0.465	0.551	0.536	0.963	0.340	0.507
Breusch-Godfrey LM test for autocorrelation, Prob>chi2	0.395	0.494	0.486	0.960	0.311	0.447

Standard errors in parentheses
Notes: Three, two, and one asterisks denote statistical significance at 1, 5, and 10 percent levels, respectively.

fuel, neither of the sanctions dummies are significant; the tests and sanctions had no effect on trade in these items.[17] The study returns below to the question of whether the sanctions might have wider signaling or economic affect by interrupting trade in weapons with other countries. Yet the evidence is consistent with an interpretation that China has effectively compensated for the loss of trade from other sources.

North-South Trade

Figure 6 provides an overview of North-South trade since its very modest inception in 1989 through 2010. A pattern emerges that is similar in some respects to China–North Korea trade, with a relatively constant level of trade through 1998, followed by steady growth through the Kim Dae-jung administration and a more dramatic inflection under Roh Moo-hyun. This inflection was driven in no small measure by aid—primarily food and fertilizer—and two major investment projects: the tourist complex at Mt. Kumgang and the Kaesong Industrial Complex, the export processing zone that began to generate meaningful levels of exports from 2005.

Despite the Roh administration's reputation as a relentless advocate of engagement, trade was briefly interrupted in 2006 by the missile

Figure 6. South Korea's Trade with North Korea, 1990–2010

USD, Millions

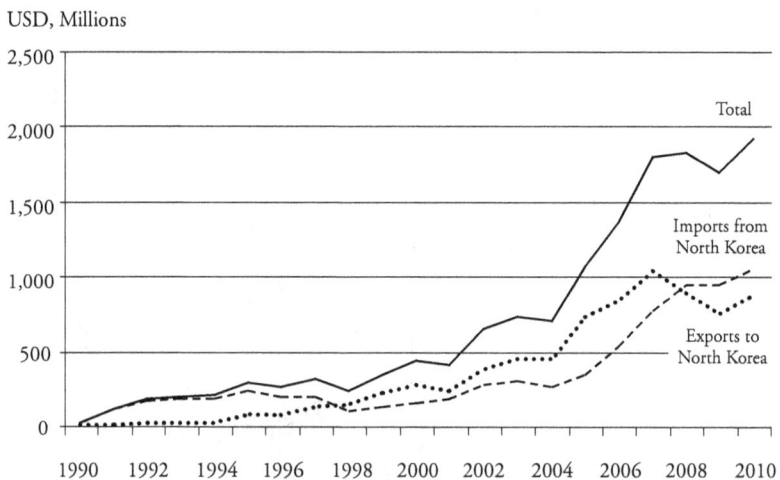

Source: Korean Statistical Information Service—North Korea (http://www.kosis.kr/bukhan).

tests (although not enough to even be visible in a figure showing annual trade data, or in econometric tests not reported here; see Noland
2009b). But bilateral trade quickly resumed in 2007, following the
resumption of the Six Party Talks and the location of more enterprises
in the Kaesong Industrial Complex.

From the beginning, North-South trade has had a strong aid and
noncommercial component. Aid was an important component of Kim
Dae-jung's Sunshine Policy, but became even more firmly institutionalized under Roh Moo-hyun. The Mt. Kumgang tourist project and the
Kaesong Industrial Complex have involved not only private companies,
but also substantial government subsidies. Both the Kim Dae-jung and
Roh Moo-hyun administrations argued that economic engagement
through such projects might moderate North Korean behavior and
provide a means to leverage reform in North Korea. Yet, for both political reasons and political economy reasons—the significance of the
projects to the firms that invested in them, including Hyundai-Asan
and the labor-intensive enterprises in Kaesong—the projects came to
have significance for the South as well, generating a kind of "reverse
leverage" on North Korea's part. Despite pressures to respond to the
2006 missile and nuclear tests by reexamining the Kaesong project,
the Roh administration chose to largely insulate this experiment from
high politics.

Figure 7 divides South Korea's exports to the North into three categories: aid, commercial trade, and cooperation projects (primarily Mt.
Kumgang and the Kaesong Industrial Complex).[18] Between 1995 and
2007—the peak of bilateral trade—South Korea's aid and economic
cooperation activities at times accounted for almost 60 percent of total
trade and have averaged more than 40 percent of trade over the "engagement" period. While the Bush administration periodically attempted
to corral support for a more confrontational posture toward the North,
both the Kim Dae-jung and Roh Moo-hyun administrations remained
committed to a relatively unconditional form of assistance, in which
both aid and cooperation projects were extended with virtually no political strings attached beyond a willingness to participate in an increasingly institutionalized set of North-South consultations.

The election of December 2007 fundamentally changed the nature of North-South economic relations. The Lee Myung-bak administration moved toward a more conditional concept of engagement, in

Figure 7. South Korean Exports to North Korea by Type, 1993–2009

USD, Millions

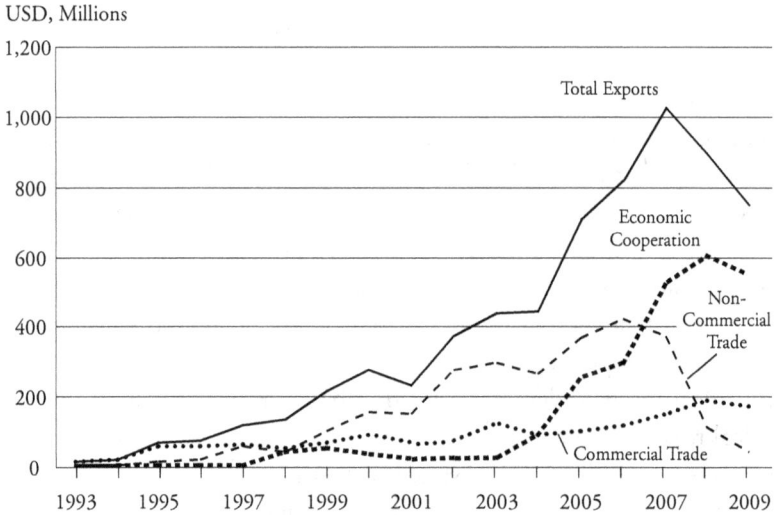

Sources: Ministry of Unification, Republic of Korea (http://www.unikorea.go.kr) and Korean Statistical Information Service—North Korea (http://www.kosis.kr/bukhan).

which expanded trade, investment, and even humanitarian assistance would follow rather than anticipate progress on the nuclear question. As Figures 6 and 7 suggest, these were not empty threats, although the increase in trade in 2010 is surprising given the events of the year. From the outset of his administration, humanitarian assistance was virtually eliminated. Following the sinking of the *Cheonan* in March 2010, commercial trade outside of the Kaesong Industrial Complex was sanctioned as well, although the administration showed a reluctance to shut down the Kaesong experiment. Following the shelling of Yeonpyeong Island in November 2010, trade outside of Kaesong was embargoed altogether, foreshadowing a future decline. Nonetheless, for much of the second nuclear crisis, the differences in US and South Korean approaches toward North Korea were clearly visible in the trade data.

Economic Diplomacy and the Six Party Talks under the Bush Administration

In this section, the focus moves from broad structural constraints on economic diplomacy toward North Korea to an overview of the role economic inducements and sanctions played in the Six Party Talks through their breakdown in 2008. The following section pushes the narrative forward into the Obama administration.[19] The narrative follows the work of Nincic (2005) and an extensive body of analysis on North Korea by Sigal (1998, 2002, 2005, 2009, 2010) that considers whether inducements and constraints generate cooperative or uncooperative, escalatory responses. In short, do such policy measures "work"?

The evidence in the following sections is outlined in Table 4; a broader overview of US sanctions efforts is contained in Appendix 4. In general, the evidence provides little support for the claim that hard-line policies or sanctions worked; to the contrary, they tended to generate escalatory responses from North Korea. As already noted, the coordination problem in orchestrating wide-ranging commercial sanctions, and the political imperviousness of the regime even when they were successfully coordinated. So-called "smart sanctions" (Cortright and Lopez 2002) did not appear to fare much better. Sanctions on weapons sales and particularly

The evidence provides little support for the claim that hard-line policies or sanctions worked

financial sanctions appear to have had surprisingly wide-ranging effects on both commercial trade and foreign accounts under the leadership's control. However, these material or economic effects do not automatically translate into the desired political response. Highly targeted sanctions only influenced the negotiations when coupled with a willingness to negotiate and offer new inducements that went beyond the lifting of existing restrictions.

However, this finding with respect to sanctions does not imply that inducements routinely worked either. The extension of inducements faced a host of credibility and sequencing problems as well.

A central issue of contention throughout the negotiations was whether inducements would be extended in advance of, simultaneously with, or only after North Korea had fulfilled stipulated obligations. Given the belief on both sides that important commitments had not been met in the past,[20] the offer of inducements was less likely to be credible if promised only after the completion of the corresponding

Table 4. Economic Statecraft in the Six Party Talks

	Economic and other inducements	Sanctions and constraints	North Korean response
Pre-crisis. January 2001–October 2002	Food aid. Oil shipments under Agreed Framework. Internal discussion of prospective benefits, but based on widened agenda.	Assertion of right to pre-empt against proliferators. Unwillingness to negotiate.	Proposal to negotiate a wide-ranging settlement, June 2003.
From the onset of the crisis to the Six Party Talks. October 2003–August 2004		Suspension of HFO shipments under Agreed Framework. Initiation of Proliferation Security Initiative Strengthening of illicit activities initiatives. "Tailored containment."	Restatement of willingness to negotiate followed by escalation (ejection of IAEA inspectors, withdrawal from NPT, reprocessing of spent fuel).
First three rounds of Six Party Talks. August 2003–January 2005	First offer of inducements at 3rd round of talks, June 2004. Offer of security guarantees, but economic inducements would follow North Korean compliance.	Continuation of existing initiatives.	Proposed exchange, with economic inducements for declaratory commitments and to precede irreversible North Korean actions. Dismantlement only with provision of LWRs. 4th round of talks do not materialize.
Through the "roadmap" agreements. January 2005–October 2007	Statement of Principles offers broad economic quid pro quos, including prospective lifting of sanctions, aid, normalization, and discussion of LWRs. South Korea provides electricity. Resolution of BDA case permits February and October 2007 agreements, which offer tightly coupled economic inducements in the form of oil shipments.	Refinement of Illicit Activities Initiative, BDA and other financial sanctions.	Escalatory response to BDA action, including missile and nuclear tests in 2006. Settlement of BDA issues, followed by return to negotiations and February and October 2007 agreements.
Implementation. October 2007–January 2009	HFO shipments, food aid, and initial steps toward lifting of sanctions conditional on North Korean performance, including with respect to verification.	US chooses not to rescind North Korea's designation as a state sponsor of terrorism as a result of conflict over verification.	Mixed compliance. Most disablement steps completed, but questionable declaration of nuclear activities and programs. Initially accepts compromise with US on verification, but escalates in response to US reversal on terrorism list and ultimately quits the talks.

obligation. As the North Koreans insisted throughout the negotiations, they should proceed on the basis of "words for words (or 'commitments for commitments'), actions for actions."

However, North Korean proposals did not necessarily conform to this injunction, creating parallel credibility problems. Inducements were periodically demanded simply to talk, in exchange for declaratory statements of intent, or to take actions that were easily reversible, most notably a "freeze" of existing activities. North Korea also sought discrete payments for highly disaggregated actions—a variant of the "salami" tactic—with the effect that important stages in the denuclearization process were effectively put off into the distant future. In the interim, North Korea retained its nuclear deterrent.

These credibility problems were related, in part, to the nature of the inducements (and obligations) on offer: their specificity and the time frame over which they could be implemented. At the most tangible end of the inducements spectrum were outright transfers, such as the delivery of fuel oil, electricity, food, or even cash, as occurred in the context of the 2000 North-South summit and, most recently, during 2007–2008. These measures provided clear and tangible benefits. Cash payments, in particular, were also fungible and could thus be used for core regime objectives, even military ones.

Complex projects such as the construction of light water reactors (LWRs) involve a much more protracted time frame, with ample opportunity for things to go wrong. The Agreed Framework stipulated clearly that "upon receipt of US assurances for the provision of LWRs and for arrangements for interim energy alternatives, the DPRK will freeze its graphite-moderated reactors and related facilities and will eventually dismantle these reactors and related facilities." However, the agreement also stipulated that "dismantlement of the DPRK's graphite-moderated reactors and related facilities will be completed when the LWR project is completed," and not before. For critics of the Agreed Framework in the United States, Korea, and Japan, the Korean Peninsula Energy Development Organization (KEDO) consortium had expended extraordinary resources without achieving any irreversible commitments from the North Koreans. When political relations soured, North Korea could "flip the switch" and once again extract plutonium from the spent fuel rods.

An additional problem with some inducements is that they are likely to have only ambiguous economic effects, a fact of which the North Koreans are no doubt perfectly aware. Despite North Korean statements that the lifting of sanctions is a crucial signal of US intent, the material effect of lifting sanctions will depend both on complementary economic policies in North Korea and on the reaction of private actors, who might still be deterred from trade and investment as a result of the general uncertainty surrounding North Korea's policy intentions. Similarly, admission into international financial institutions (IFIs) does not necessarily ensure lending because of the conditional nature of IFI programs. The problem with these inducements is even more pronounced if it is believed that important actors in North Korea are simply seeking delay or are indifferent, or even hostile, to increased trade, investment, or involvement with the IFIs in the first place. These concerns no doubt explain the preference of the regime for tangible and fungible resource transfers over inducements that have only indirect—even if potentially significant—economic effects.

However, the problems with respect to inducements were not simply a function of the nature of the goods on offer; they also reflected the unwillingness of North Korea to comply with certain stipulations, including a full declaration of its existing nuclear activities and submission to a robust verification regime. By late 2008—when Kim Jong-il was believed to have had a stroke—North Korean behavior was consistent with either a conscious effort to delay the entire denuclearization process, perhaps waiting for the Obama administration to take office, or with purely internal dynamics that made decision making on the topic difficult.

Prior to the Crisis: January 2001–October 2002
The deep divisions that existed within the first Bush administration with respect to its North Korea policy have now been thoroughly documented (Mazarr 2007, Pritchard 2007, Chinoy 2008). On the one hand, there were some signs of a willingness to engage, or at least abide by formal commitments. Inducements under the Agreed Framework—fuel oil shipments to North Korea and efforts through KEDO to complete the long-delayed construction of the promised light water reactors (LWR)—remained intact despite efforts from within the administration to kill them (Chinoy 2008, 75–77), as did the provision

of food aid. Secretary of State Colin Powell favored a continuation of the talks initiated by the Clinton administration and, following the completion of a policy review in June 2001, appeared to gain the authority to proceed.[21]

However, hawks within the administration bitterly opposed the Agreed Framework or any negotiations with Pyongyang at all. The president himself sent distinctly mixed signals with respect to the utility of engagement, most notably in his repudiation of Powell's stated intention to pursue the Clinton negotiations on missiles, in the open clash with President Kim Dae-jung over the utility of the Sunshine Pol-

> *President Bush sent distinctly mixed signals about the utility of engagement*

icy during his state visit in March 2001, and in the infamous "Axis of Evil" comment in the 2002 State of the Union address.

Moreover, both the agenda and the modality of engagement marked sharp departures from the Clinton era that seemed almost designed to fail. The differences in approach are clearly visible in a speech by Colin Powell before the Asia Society in June 2002. This speech reflected the findings of both the 2001 policy review and a second policy review in early 2002 called the "bold approach."[22] Although nominally endorsing the "sunshine approach," the speech made progress in bilateral relations conditional on a number of prior actions by the North Koreans: on humanitarian issues, conventional force deployments, missiles, and the country's obligations under both the Agreed Framework and the Nuclear Non-Proliferation Treaty (NPT). The earlier policy review had also put human rights on the agenda. A particular point of controversy was the timing of International Atomic Energy Agency (IAEA) inspections, which the United States and the agency sought to push up in time.

Internal discussions in the United States did consider possible benefits. Measures under discussion included replacing the light water nuclear reactors promised under the Agreed Framework with thermal and hydropower plants, aid for infrastructure, humanitarian assistance in the form of food aid and construction of schools and hospitals, and support for admitting North Korea into the World Bank and Asian Development Bank (Sigal 2005). But these were publicly outlined only in the most vague terms (for example, Powell's speech offered that "the United States is prepared to take important steps to help North Korea move its relations with the US toward normalcy"), and would in any case come only after satisfactory steps were taken on the US agenda.

In addition to the mixed signals with respect to North Korea policy itself, September 11 triggered a much more aggressive posture toward proliferators, including the assertion of a right of preemption.[23] When coupled with the administration's pointed unwillingness to reiterate the Clinton administration's statement of peaceful intent, and with public speeches by members of the administration outlining perceived North Korean derogations, it was certainly plausible for Pyongyang—and the North Korean military—to draw the conclusion that the United States had hostile intent that required deterrence.[24] The invasion of Iraq, which occurred precisely as the crisis was breaking, no doubt only deepened these concerns.

Did the Bush administration's hardened stance have an effect? The North Koreans responded negatively to the substance of the policy review, and particularly the introduction of additional issues and demands for further inspections at Yongbyon. Pyongyang sought to focus any discussion around full implementation of the Agreed Framework, including the completion of the light water reactors (LWR) and compensation for lost electricity. Nonetheless, they also signaled a willingness to negotiate.[25] These overtures were ignored.

It was not until the Association of Southeast Asian Nations (ASEAN) Regional Forum meeting in July 2002—a year and half into office—that Secretary of State Colin Powell communicated US willingness to send an envoy to Pyongyang to outline the "bold approach." The debate within the administration centered on whether the HEU issue should be folded into this broader agenda of the policy review and "bold approach," or whether it should be the primary focus of talks. Tightly instructed, Assistant Secretary of State James A. Kelly's October visit hewed to the second approach.

From the Onset of the Crisis to the Six Party Talks: October 2002– August 2003

To this day, what happened during the Kelly visit remains the subject of dispute even to those who were present. Did the North Koreans admit to having a uranium enrichment (HEU) program, did they only claim the right to have one, or did they deny it altogether (Pritchard 2007, 34–40)? And even if they did deny it, was an opportunity missed because of tight instructions that prohibited the United States from signaling a willingness to negotiate?[26] Although there is still debate about how far along the program was, the fact that at least some technology had been transferred from the Pakistanis, including centrifuges, now seems

What happened during the Kelly visit remains the subject of dispute even to those who were present

beyond dispute. Moreover, such transfers took place well before the Bush administration came to office.[27] Such transfers would have constituted a clear breach of a number of North Korea's international commitments, including the Nuclear Non-Proliferation Treaty, the 1992 Joint [North-South] Declaration on the Denuclearization of the Korean Peninsula, and the Agreed Framework.

But the key issue is not simply whether the North Koreans had a program or how far along it was, but what the United States intended to do about it. In the aftermath of the confrontational visit, the administration exerted strong pressure on both Japan and South Korea to concur with a KEDO resolution condemning the HEU program as a violation of the Agreed Framework and cutting off fuel oil shipments. The North Korean response to this effort to impose costs was generally escalatory rather than compromising. In October, North Korea proposed the negotiation of an agreement that would resolve all outstanding nuclear issues in return for three concessions: respect for North Korean sovereignty; a binding US commitment to nonaggression; and a pledge that the United States not "hamper" the country's economic development, presumably a reference to the lifting of sanctions. Interestingly, this proposal made explicit reference to the economic reforms of 2002 as a sign of the regime's good intent.[28]

This proposal was revived by the North Koreans following the cutoff of oil shipments in November. When the United States failed to respond, Pyongyang quickly escalated. In December 2002, Pyongyang asked the International Atomic Energy Agency (IAEA) to unseal the Yongbyon facilities, and when the agency asked the government to reconsider, the inspectors were ejected. An IAEA board statement condemning the move was followed by North Korea's formal renunciation of its obligations under the nonproliferation treaty on January 10, 2003. Shortly thereafter, the regime resumed reprocessing from spent nuclear fuel rods that had been stored in North Korea under the Agreed Framework, and were subject to IAEA inspection, but which had not yet been removed from the country. North Korea also took steps to generate new fissile material by refueling and restarting the reactor. At several points during the spring, the North Koreans either stated or hinted that they already had a nuclear capability, or that they saw it as their right to develop one (for example, Pritchard 2007, 65).

The United States subsequently undertook a variety of other actions designed to pressure the North Koreans to reconsider, including the mobilization of military force in the region. Two sets of measures that were to have more enduring significance were the initiation of the Proliferation Security Initiative (May 31, 2003), a multilateral effort to cooperate around the interdiction of trade in weapons of mass destruction (WMD)–related materials, and the ongoing strengthening of interagency efforts to deter and stop North Korean engagement in illicit activities, including counterfeiting, the drug trade, and the financial transactions and money-laundering associated with the country's weapons trade.[29] At least in the short run, these measures had little concrete effect. Effectively stymied, the administration undertook a third policy review in which divergent strategies, from engagement to regime change, were tabled (Funabashi 2007, 138–139; Chinoy 2008, 145–147). The chosen middle-ground approach—"tailored containment"—explicitly eschewed any direct negotiation with North Korea, while seeking to orchestrate economic and political pressure against the regime (with some openly hoping that the regime would collapse as a result).

Thanks to papers released by Donald Rumsfeld, interesting insights are illuminated concerning the precise logic underlying the "tailored containment" approach, at least as viewed by the secretary of defense.[30] In a memo dated December 26, 2002, with a wide distribution among the top leadership of the administration,[31] Rumsfeld responds to the expulsion of IAEA inspectors by arguing against negotiations. "Getting to the table is what Pyongyang seeks; for us to grant it in response to the latest nuclear provocations would only reinforce Pyongyang's weak hand and prove that bad behavior pays." Rumsfeld argues for aggressive economic-cum-political diplomacy, including the pursuit of sanctions against missile exports through the IAEA and UN; cutting off funds that North Korea receives from abroad, including from pro–North Korean groups in Japan (the Chosen Soren was mentioned by name); and "pressing China and Russia to ratchet up diplomatic pressure and constrict economic aid and development projects." The ultimate objective of these sanctions was to "train Kim Jong-il to understand that blackmail tactics that worked with the previous administration will no longer work."

Ironically, such a strategy required a multilateral approach. The Six Party Talks had their origin in a trilateral meeting hosted by Beijing in April 2003. The expansion to six parties appeared to serve American interests by providing a venue through which the five parties could coordinate—and pressure—the North to abandon its weapons program. However, as already seen, the new South Korean government of Roh Moo-hyun had doubts about the utility of pressure and was wedded to a wide-ranging engagement approach. Despite recurrent frustrations with North Korea, China shared these

> *The Six Party Talks forced the Bush administration to consider the inducements it would be willing to offer*

views with respect to strategy, as has now been widely documented (International Crisis Group 2006, 2009; Snyder 2009). Russia had doubts about the utility of pressure as well (Funabashi 2007, 166–196; Toloraya 2008). Rather than marshaling collective pressure on North Korea, the Six Party Talks gradually forced the Bush administration to consider the inducements it would be willing to offer for a settlement.

The First Three Rounds of the Six Party Talks: August 2003–January 2005

The United States did not come into the first round of the Six Party Talks (August 27–29, 2003) with a negotiating strategy, but rather with a list of demands. These became embodied in the acronym CVID: the United States was seeking a *complete* (meaning plutonium and HEU), *verifiable* (meaning a return to the NPT and IAEA inspections), *irreversible dismantlement* of all facilities at Yongbyon (distinct from the Agreed Framework, which had frozen North Korea's nuclear program, but left it intact). Although inducements for compliance were not made explicit—in part because of ongoing disagreements within the administration[32]—the sequencing of them was clear: any concessions from the United States would come only after these actions had been completed.

The opening North Korean statement, which mirrored the North Korean proposal at the three-party talks in April, suggested that Pyongyang was willing to negotiate to get to CVID, but it had a very clear view of how the sequencing of inducements would have to unfold to reach a credible agreement.[33] As a first step, the North Koreans would declare their intention to abandon their nuclear program in return for Washington's resumption of fuel oil supplies and expanded humanitarian food aid. In the second phase, North Korea would freeze its nuclear activities—but not dismantle them—and allow inspections if the United States signed a legally binding nonaggression treaty and compensated the North for lost energy supplies. It is a revealing insight into North Korean calculations that they themselves characterized these exchanges as a "freeze for reward" (Koh 2004). In the third step, Pyongyang would accommodate US concerns about missiles, in return for establishing diplomatic relations. Finally, at the point of completion of the two light water reactors (LWR) promised under the Agreed Framework, the North Koreans would verifiably dismantle the Yongbyon facilities. As with US proposals, the North Korean approach frontloaded inducements while delaying irreversible actions until the distant future.

With US negotiators given little discretion to negotiate, the first talks ended with such limited progress that the Chinese had to extend bilateral inducements of their own to get the North Koreans to even return to the next round (Funabashi 2007, 320–321). This became a pattern, as China, South Korea (through the Kaesong project), and Japan (through a second Koizumi-Kim summit) extended various inducements to North Korea, both to improve the prospects of the talks and for diplomatic objectives altogether independent of the Six Party process.

The second round of talks (February 25–28, 2004) was similarly hamstrung by disagreements over the nature and sequencing of concessions. Not until the third round of talks (June 23–26, 2004) did the United States place an offer on the table, and it constituted a virtual mirror image of the North Korean approach. North Korean commitments were heavily front-loaded, while American inducements would not be forthcoming until progress was made on a wide agenda of bilateral issues. In return for a North Korean statement of its willingness to dismantle all nuclear programs, South Korea and Japan would resume shipments of heavy fuel oil in line with the Agreed Framework commitments. The North would institute a freeze on all nuclear activities and provide the five parties with a detailed plan for disabling, dismantling, and eliminating all of its nuclear activities, including its HEU program, existing stocks of fissile material, weapons, and components; all of this work would take place under the auspices of international inspections. Once agreement on the plan was reached, the United States and others would provide security assurances, but other economic inducements, such as meeting longer-run energy needs or removing sanctions, would be phased and subject to further negotiation. The path to normalization was more distant still and would require progress on the widened agenda of the June 2001 policy review and "bold approach." The North Koreans stalled, and the fourth round of talks scheduled to take place prior to September 2004 failed to materialize.

Bush's Second Term I: Through the "Roadmap" Agreements of 2007
The "Initial Actions for the Implementation of the Joint Statement" of February 13, 2007, outlined a series of very short-run measures designed to build confidence based on a tightly scripted exchange of concessions. In the language of the agreement, "the Parties agreed to take coordinated steps to implement the Joint Statement in a phased manner in line with the principle of 'actions for actions.'"

In the first 60 days, a freeze on Yongbyon—an agreement to "shut down and seal [the facility] for the purpose of eventual abandonment"—and the return of IAEA inspectors were to be exchanged for delivery of oil. North Korea also agreed to begin discussions on a declaration of its activities, although not to complete it or provide it in full. In response, the United States committed to set in motion a number of diplomatic processes, although not necessarily to complete them: to "start" bilateral talks aimed at normalization; to "begin" the process of removing North Korea from the list of state sponsors of terrorism; and to "advance the process" of lifting sanctions under the Trading with the Enemy Act. During the first phase and the next phase, a complete declaration of all nuclear programs and disablement of all existing nuclear facilities would be exchanged for economic, energy, and humanitarian assistance up to the equivalent of one million tons of heavy fuel oil (HFO). But this large package—in excess of what was offered under the Agreed Framework—would depend on the full disablement of all nuclear facilities; in the short run, the only inducement on offer was a shipment of 50,000 tons of HFO.

The October 2007 agreement—the "Second-Phase Actions for the Implementation of the September 2005 Joint Statement"—reiterated these commitments and set out a more precise timetable and further details on these exchanges. The agreement appears to state clearly that the disablement of the reactor, reprocessing plant, and fuel fabrication facility would be completed by the end of 2007, and a full declaration would be provided. The October agreement also states explicitly that removing North Korea from the list of state sponsors of terrorism would be conditional on actions with respect to disablement. Not stated explicitly, although implied by the "actions for actions" approach, is that the North Koreans expected disablement to also be phased to the provision of the HFO inducements, suggesting a timetable that would likely run well past the deadline of the end of 2007.

Bush's Second Term II: Actions for Actions?

Did the "actions for actions" approach work? The February agreement to freeze the North's nuclear facilities was delayed as a result of technical difficulties in resolving the Banco Delta Asia (BDA) issue, but oil shipments commenced in July, and the freeze was in place by October 2007 when second-phase actions were to commence.[34] North Korea began implementing the October 3 agreement by shutting down the five-megawatt nuclear reactor at Yongbyon, and although it missed the year-end deadline for disablement—completing 8 of 11 steps designed to make it inoperable for at least a year—this deviation was partly technical and not viewed as particularly serious on the part of the United States. The North Koreans would subsequently modulate their disablement efforts, complaining about the pace that fuel oil was being delivered.[35]

The declaration and the linked issue of verification, however, posed stumbling blocks that led to the final collapse of the talks. The October agreement required North Korea to provide a "complete and correct declaration of all its nuclear programs." However, an early declaration provided in November fell well short of US and other intelligence estimates of the likely stock of fissile material, was lacking in detail, and made no mention of either HEU or proliferation activities. These activities had become an increasing issue of concern following the Israeli bombing of a reactor, which had been constructed with North Korean support, in the Syrian Des-

North Korea's failure to fully declare its nuclear programs and the issue of verification led to the collapse of the talks

ert in September 2007. Following three further rounds of negotiations in early 2008, the United States and North Korea reached an agreement in Singapore in April 2008, under which North Korea promised a new declaration of the plutonium-based program, the United States would provide a bill of particulars on its suspicions with respect to proliferation activities and HEU—which the North Koreans continued to deny—and these concerns would be confidentially "acknowledged." A massive compilation of documents was delivered to the United States in May and formally to China as chair of the Six Party Talks in June.

Not coincidentally, a major food aid package with the United States was finalized at the same time, suggesting a tacit linkage between much-needed humanitarian assistance and progress on the talks. The United States responded as required by lifting restrictions applied to North Korea associated with the Trading with the Enemy Act and through President George W. Bush's formal notice to congress of his intention to remove Pyongyang from the list of state sponsors of terrorism after 45 days. During the July 2008 round of talks, the six parties each agreed to fulfill "in parallel" their agreed commitments with respect to HFO shipments (or equivalents) and to complete disablement by the end of October.

The statement of principles of September 2005 made reference to the fact that denuclearization would be "verifiable" and that North Korea would return to the NPT and IAEA inspections. However, the management of verification issues had been delegated to the nuclear working group in the February 2007 agreement, implying that it was not a component of the first two phases of implementation. Following bilateral negotiations on the issue, the parties released a joint communiqué on July 12 outlining broad principles, including agreement that at least the initial inspection mechanism would involve experts from the six parties, with the IAEA limited to "consultancy and assistance."

Both domestic political constraints within the United States and increasing disaffection on the part of South Korea and Japan (which refused to supply fuel oil at all because of the failure to address the abductee issue)—in short, both credibility and coordination problems—undermined the tightly scripted exchange of inducements and North Korean actions. As criticism mounted both outside and inside the administration about the integrity of the North Korean declaration and the utility of the entire Six Party process, the administration sought to mollify critics by moving verification efforts into phase two.[36] Following the July 12 joint communiqué, the United States circulated a draft of a very tough verification protocol that included full access to all materials and all sites, regardless of whether they were included in the North's declaration or not—in effect, the equivalent of the IAEA special inspections protocol. Moreover, the United States demanded that IAEA inspectors would ultimately lead the implementation of the protocol, in line with expectations stated in the September 2005 joint statement that North Korea would return "at an early date" to the NPT and to IAEA safeguards. When North Korea rejected these efforts, claiming that full verification would come only at the end of the denuclearization process, the administration chose not to rescind North Korea's designation as a state sponsor of terrorism on August 11, at the end of the 45-day period.

These events occurred exactly at the time that Kim Jong-il was subsequently believed to have suffered a stroke, compounding the difficulty of reaching any agreement. On August 26, a foreign ministry statement announced that North Korea would stop and then reverse the disablement process at Yongbyon and, in a thinly veiled reference to the military, restore facilities "as strongly requested by its relevant institutions."[37] On September 24, it removed IAEA seals and surveillance cameras from its reprocessing facility and restricted international inspectors from its reactor site in a virtual replay of the events of early 2003. South Korean intelligence leaks also suggested that North Korea was restoring an undeclared underground nuclear site at Punggye and the ballistic test site in Musudan, suggesting a hard-line response to the US change in course that would extend into the Obama administration.

Realizing that the entire Six Party process was now in jeopardy, the administration reversed course and sent the head of the US delegation, Christopher Hill, to Pyongyang in early October to negotiate a face-saving protocol that would permit Pyongyang to be taken off the terrorism list.[38] But nearly a month after this last-minute concession was granted, North Korea questioned its precise terms with respect to the taking of samples, once again providing an entry point for critics of the deal. Last-minute efforts to save a deal through two further rounds of negotiations in December proved unsuccessful. The United States believed that the North Koreans had reneged on verbal assurances of allowing verification that had been given in October, and stated that further energy assistance under the agreement would not be forthcoming, effectively ending the implementation process.

A Reprise: Inducements and Constraints in the Six Party Talks

Several conclusions emerge from this narrative. First, the history of the talks confirms the coordination problems noted in the previous section. The United States had limited success in turning the Six Party Talks into a five-party cartel that would use economic-cum-political pressure to bring North Korea to the table and elicit concessions. China's commitment to deep engagement was a constant, and it exercised influence both within the Six Party Talks and through its capacity to influence UN Security Council action in 2006. Japan (roughly through the second Koizumi-Kim summit in 2004) and South Korea (though the end of the Roh administration in 2007) also sought to engage North Korea, even at times when the talks were not progressing. As Rumsfeld himself was forced to admit in a memo to the president in October 2006—only days before the first nuclear test—"it is not only difficult, but possibly impossible, for the US to gain the international diplomatic support sufficient to impose the leverage on Iran and/or North Korea required to cause them to discontinue their nuclear programs."[39]

But the strategy of pressuring North Korea was not only futile, it was also counterproductive. North Korea responded to both military threats and economic pressure by accelerating their pursuit of weapons, most notably in early 2003, in 2006,

> *The strategy of pressuring North Korea was both futile and counterproductive*

and again in 2008–2009, leading ultimately to the second round of missile and nuclear tests in the first year of the Obama administration. Moreover, although purely internal political dynamics cannot be discounted, it is plausible that the broader shift in North Korean politics away from reform and toward greater military dominance could be attributed to the deteriorating security environment following the onset of the crisis.

This conclusion about the counterproductive nature of sanctions appears to pertain with respect to "smart sanctions" as well. Despite the fact that the United States did not trade extensively with North Korea, it was able to leverage its centrality in international financial systems to constrain financial institutions in third countries and, thus, affect North Korea's commercial transactions. There is evidence that the BDA actions had an effect because of the weight that the North Koreans put on them in the resumption of negotiations. But these apparent gains must be put in context. The timing of the BDA announcement undermined the momentum of the September joint statement and resulted in a suspension of the talks for over a year, during which the North Koreans tested nuclear weapons. The BDA sanctions only had effect because the United States was willing to resolve the issue and resume negotiations.

But the fact that sanctions did not appear to have an effect does not mean that inducements worked. On the positive side of the ledger, US willingness to offer inducements was crucial to the negotiations leading to the 2005 breakthrough, the resumption of talks in 2006, and the two road-map agreements of 2007.

But what about implementation of the agreements? Christopher Hill's strategy in 2008 was to focus on the inducements required to stop production of plutonium in Yongbyon through an agreement on disabling the facility, while finessing the issues of proliferation, HEU, accumulated stocks of fissile material, and the weapons themselves. Once the North Koreans saw the benefits to be gained from making concessions, and once trust was built, it was hoped that they would then be willing to strike deals on these questions as well.

But it is not clear that North Korea was willing to deal on these questions, either because of more permanent changes that had taken place in the North Korean political economy or because of the particular succession issues that surfaced following Kim Jong-il's stroke in

August 2008. If taken in good faith, the deal made with respect to pro-liferation and HEU could be treated as an acknowledgment that North Korea had engaged in such behavior in the past, but would not do so in the future. But the bitter fight over verification, though technically not a part of phase-two implementation, raised broader questions about North Korean intentions. American negotiators, at least, believed that the final breakdown in December was the result of North Korea reneging on verbal assurances concerning verification granted in October.

A less charitable interpretation of the events of 2008 suggests that either North Korea was divided on the issue or simply engaged in strategic deception. North Korea never officially acknowledged its proliferation activities—despite overwhelming evidence on the Syrian reactor—or its HEU program. Even had the 2007 agreements been fully implemented, a prolonged round of further negotiations—and side payments—would have been required to address verification, reentry into the

> *The least charitable interpretation is that the North Koreans sought to maintain a nuclear deterrent*

NPT, the readmission of IAEA inspectors, the question of existing stocks of fissile material and weapons, as well as HEU and nuclear cooperation with Syria, Iran, and other states. At each stage, the question of inducements for North Korean compliance would have come up. During these negotiations, North Korea would have effectively maintained a nuclear capability. The least charitable interpretation is that the North Koreans simply sought to maintain at least a minimal nuclear deterrent.

It is impossible based on the evidence to distinguish between these two different interpretations; they are observationally equivalent. But the North Korean reaction must be read not only against the evidence of American efforts to introduce the verification issue, on which North Korea ultimately relented, but also on domestic developments in North Korea, particularly in the wake of Kim Jong-il's stroke. As has been argued, those developments were by no means in the direction of reform and opening, but, rather, were moving in the opposite direction altogether, culminating in the disastrous currency reform of late 2009. Evidence for this less charitable interpretation can be found by outlining the developments of the first two years of the Obama administration.

The Obama Administration, 2009–2010

The Obama administration came to office committed to a strategy toward its adversaries that was almost diametrically opposed to that pursued by the first Bush administration. At least in a general way, the Obama administration signaled a willingness to engage North Korea. Did this strategy have effect? The answer is "no." The North Korean response to the new administration was highly provocative: quickly testing both a long-range missile and a second nuclear device and withdrawing "permanently" from the Six Party Talks.

The administration pursued a two-track policy in response. On the one hand, it orchestrated wide-ranging multilateral sanctions against North Korea through the UN Security Council and aggressively pursued its implementation. On the other hand, it sought to balance these constraints with a stated willingness to reengage through the Six Party Talks on the basis of the September 2005 statement of principles. This willingness to engage did not involve the offer of any new incentives; to the contrary, the administration specifically rejected such measures. But it did repeatedly restate the benefits of reaching a settlement and the willingness to meet all US obligations under the September 2005 agreement.

Through the sinking of the *Cheonan*, this two-track strategy—dubbed "strategic patience," on the premise that the onus for a resumption of the talks falls largely on North Korea—did not succeed in bringing North Korea back to the negotiating table. At each step that sanctions were imposed, North Korea responded by escalating tensions. But North Korea also pursued a "two-track" policy of signaling a willingness to negotiate. The key problem in restarting the negotiations was once again a sequencing issue, disguised as a debate about venue. The United States—and the other five parties—insisted on a resumption of the Six Party Talks on the basis of the joint statement of September 2005. North Korea eschewed the Six Party process, and sought four-party (or, ideally, three-party) talks on a "peace regime" that would replace the armistice. These talks would occur in advance of or, at best, in parallel with the Six Party process. In the interim, North Korea would remain—de facto if not de jure—a nuclear power.

In March 2010, Pyongyang undertook one of the more egregious provocations of the post–Korean War period by sinking a South Korean naval vessel, the *Cheonan*, resulting in the loss of 46 lives. American policy was subsequently tied to South Korea's response, which raised the hurdle for restarting the Six Party Talks to include a resolution of the *Cheonan* issue. No sooner had the Lee Myung-bak administration signaled a tentative willingness to move beyond the *Cheonan* question in the fall of 2010 than the North Koreas undertook the shelling of Yeonpyeong Island, sovereign territory of South Korea.[40] The prospects for negotiations dimmed still further as the United States, South Korea, and Japan focused their attention on reestablishing the credibility of the military deterrent on the Korean peninsula.

> *One of Pyongyang's more egregious provocations was the 2010 sinking of the* **Cheonan**

As in the past, the policy debate rotated several conflicting interpretations, each with conflicting assumptions about what role economic statecraft might play.

Leon V. Sigal (2009) argues that North Korea's behavior in the first half of 2009 was largely a response to the failure of the negotiations in late 2008. Just as North Korea had taken an escalatory response to the cutoff of HFO shipments in 2002, it responded similarly to the joint decision of the United States, South Korea, and Japan to suspend HFO shipments in December 2008. These problems were compounded by the failure of the Obama administration to engage North Korea with sufficient alacrity and by the "crime and punishment" strategy of imposing sanctions in the wake of the missile test of April.[41] The bellicose language and the missile and nuclear tests by the North Koreans were, according to Sigal, simply tactics designed to increase bargaining leverage. Nonetheless, the September 2005 deal was still within reach if the United States and other five parties engaged to achieve it.

A second variant of this argument sees the North Koreans as bargaining, but acknowledges that North Korea severely miscalculated the international reaction to the missile and nuclear tests, and later to the sinking of the *Cheonan* and shelling of Yeonpyeong Island. As a result, North Korea may have intended to negotiate but, in fact, set in motion the sanctions-defiance spiral from which it became increasingly difficult to exit. By overplaying their hand, Pyongyang made it politically difficult, if not impossible, for the United States, South Korea, and Japan to engage.

A third alternative is that domestic political dynamics in North Korea pushed the regime toward a harder line, which hampered their ability to reach a settlement. This might have been due to growing disaffection with the Six Party process. But it might also have arisen from other domestic constraints, including short-run insecurities following Kim Jong-il's stroke in August 2008, the mounting economic difficulties the government faced, and the perceived need to show strength and boost support domestically. More pessimistically, longer-run regime dynamics might have strengthened the hand of the military, generating a more-or-less permanent "rejectionist" posture. This posture was abetted by China's ongoing willingness to provide political and economic support, a stance that was particularly clear in the "even-handed" approach Beijing took to the shelling of Yeonpyeong Island (International Crisis Group 2011). Under this interpretation, there is no deal that would be acceptable to both sides—the bargaining space has effectively collapsed—with the critical implication that North Korea has "broken out" and become a nuclear weapons state.

A final possibility is that there is continuity in North Korean policy throughout the entire crisis: the country has always been involved in some combination of blackmail and strategic deception (Bechtol 2010).

This study is inclined toward the second and particularly the third of these four alternatives: that whatever opportunities for rapprochement may have existed in the past, they closed in 2009–2010 as a result of miscalculations on North Korea's part and domestic political dynamics that made a settlement either difficult or undesirable. This interpretation would suggest that North Korea may be less affected by economic statecraft than advocates of both engagement and sanctions tend to believe. This study focuses first on the period through the sinking of the *Cheonan*, and then deals more briefly with the aftermath of that event.

> ***Whatever opportunities for rapprochement may have existed, they closed in 2009–2010***

Engagement Manquè: January 2009–March 2010

In a controversial CNN/YouTube debate in July 2007, Barack Obama answered affirmatively to a question of whether he would be willing to meet "separately, without preconditions, in the first year of [his] administration with the leaders of Iran, Syria, Venezuela, Cuba, and North Korea." Of political necessity, that position was subsequently modified—for example, by underlining that the talks would require preparation and needed to serve American interests. Nonetheless, the administration clearly signaled a willingness to engage North Korea and to build on the strategy that the Bush administration had pursued prior to the breakdown of the Six Party Talks in 2008. According to Stephen Bosworth, the president's North Korea envoy, this commitment was not only made through public statements, but also was communicated directly to North Korea in the president's first few days in office.[42]

Yet even before the missile launch, North Korean statements introduced demands that it would be physically as well as politically impossible to meet, such as removing South Korea from the US nuclear umbrella. A crucial issue that was to persist throughout 2009–2010 was the sequencing of the Six Party Talks and the process of normalizing diplomatic relations. At her nomination hearings, Secretary of State Hillary Rodham Clinton suggested—but did not in fact state—that the United States would not negotiate normalization of relations prior to complete denuclearization. The North Koreans responded furiously that normalization was not a reward for disarming and that their "status as a nuclear weapons state" would remain unchanged as long as North Korea was exposed "even to the slightest US nuclear threat."[43]

Pyongyang sharply escalated North-South tensions in early 2009 as well, abrogating all North-South agreements and claiming that the Northern Limit Line (NLL) was "null and void." Even if these statements are discounted as North Korean hyperbole or as a bargaining strategy, they appear much more bellicose than at any other phase of the negotiations.

The Obama administration's embrace of sanctions came in response to North Korea's effort to place a satellite in orbit with a three-stage "space launch vehicle." North Korea protested vigorously that it had a right to the peaceful use of outer space and was, in any case, not a state party to the Missile Technology Control Regime. These protests notwithstanding, the launch was clearly indistinguishable from an intercontinental missile test and, thus, in unambiguous violation of UNSC Resolution 1718.[44]

After efforts by Japan to secure support for a UN Security Council resolution failed, a compromise was reached on a presidential statement. Typically viewed as a weaker signal, the statement nonetheless condemned the launch as a violation of UNSC 1718, but also called on parties to fully implement their sanctions obligations under 1718 and to further "adjust" those measures through the designation of more entities and goods.

A classic escalatory cycle followed that bore a surface resemblance to the events of 2002–2003. But North Korean capabilities were now far advanced from what they had been, with a corresponding indifference to the resumption of talks. Within hours of the presidential statement, North Korea permanently withdrew from the Six Party Talks, declared all commitments under the talks as null and void, and threatened to resume the reprocessing of spent fuel rods, pursue construction of a light water reactor (LWR), and boost its nuclear deterrent.[45] The IAEA and US inspectors who had been on the ground at Yongbyon were ejected. On April 24, the UN Sanctions Committee issued the "adjustments" to 1718 requested by the presidential statement, designating three additional North Korean firms as subject to sanctions. The foreign ministry quickly affirmed that reprocessing had begun, suggested that the imposition of sanctions would constitute a nullification of the armistice, and threatened both further missile tests and a second nuclear test.

That second test came on May 25. Following a prolonged and difficult diplomatic process, the UN Security Council passed Resolution 1874 on June 12, calling on North Korea to cease and desist development of its nuclear and missile programs and to return to the Six Party Talks, the Nuclear Non-proliferation Treaty, and the International Atomic Energy Agency (IAEA) safeguards. It is worth outlining the corresponding sanctions in some detail, not only for their economic significance, but also for the strength of the political signal they sent, particularly from China.[46]

UNSC Resolution 1874 went well beyond UNSC Resolution 1718 in both the scope of products covered and in the means of enforcing the sanctions. With respect to product coverage, the new resolution did not constitute a trade embargo on North Korea or target nonmilitary commercial trade at all, and humanitarian assistance was explicitly excluded. Nonetheless, it extended the prior multilateral sanctions under UNSC Resolution 1718 beyond major weapons systems, products related to the production of weapons of mass destruction (WMD), and luxury goods to include all arms-related trade, as well as to all training or assistance related to it. The latter is particularly important because North Korea not only exports weapons systems, but also has engaged in various forms of collaboration on both missile and nuclear technologies, including with both Iran and Syria (UNSC 2010). Moreover, the resolution contained one general sanction not related to the arms trade: it calls on both international institutions and member states not to undertake new grants, financial assistance, or concessional loans to North Korea, and it asks that they maintain "vigilance" with respect to current aid programs.

The most interesting features of the resolution have to do with means of enforcement. As seen in the previous section, President Bush launched the Proliferation Security Initiative (PSI) in 2003 as a response to the onset of the crisis. The new UN Security Council resolution comes close to making the PSI a formal multilateral effort. The resolution "calls upon" (but does not require) member states to inspect all cargo on their territory, including at both seaports and airports, if it is believed to contain prohibited items. Moreover, it authorizes members to inspect vessels on the high seas or to escort them to port if there are reasonable grounds to believe that they are carrying prohibited cargo. It also precludes the provision of bunkering services to any ship suspected of prohibited trade, placing an additional constraint on any suspect ship.

An important loophole is that such interdiction must have the consent of the country under which the vessel is flagged; acting under Chapter 7, Article 41, UNSC Resolution 1874 does not authorize the use of force. If the flag state does not consent, then "the flag state shall direct the vessel to proceed to an appropriate and convenient port for the required inspection." North Korea transports some prohibited materials under its own flag, though due to the ever more dilapidated state of its fleet, it increasingly relies on foreign-flagged commercial vessels for transport. Even so, the resolution does impose constraints. Major flags of convenience, such as Panama and Liberia, are under strong pressure to comply, while failure to cooperate allows states to deny ships bunkering services. In 2009, a shadowed North Korean ship believed to be headed to Myanmar was ultimately forced to return to North Korea. Significant shipments of weapons were also interdicted in 2009 and 2010 in the United Arab Emirates, Thailand, and South Africa; as Table 5 shows, these actions were not insignificant.[47]

In addition to interdiction, the UNSC resolution explicitly provides for the use of financial means for stopping the flow of WMD-related trade. These measures were potentially more sweeping than those related to trade sanctions per se, since the resolution permit-

The 2009 Security Council resolution allows use of financial measures for stopping WMD-related trade

ted the blocking of transfers and even the freezing of any assets that "could contribute" to North Korea's weapons programs or activities. Such a provision was open to broader interpretation than trade sanctions, since it could in principle affect the finances of firms involved not only in weapons

trade, but also in dual-use technologies, inputs, or financial transactions related to such trade. Monitoring financial transactions was a more flexible instrument than designating particular firms because of the ability of North Korea to proliferate shell companies that were not technically named by the UN Sanctions Committee. As with the Banco Delta Asia (BDA) sanctions, the United States was willing to implement these measures aggressively on its own—for example, by designating new entities and individuals under existing statute and issuing an additional bank advisory with respect to North Korea following the passage of 1874.[48] The United States also engaged in active sanctions enforcement diplomacy to encourage others to do so as well. Following the passage of 1874, the United States appointed an ambassador for sanctions enforcement who traveled to the region and engaged in consultations with officials in China, Malaysia, Thailand, Singapore, and Russia on sanctions enforcement.

Finally, the resolution established a new process for overseeing the sanctions effort by creating a panel of experts. The panel would oversee the implementation of both UNSC Resolution 1718 and UNSC Resolution 1874, monitor efforts on the part of member states, and provide more independent recommendations to the UN Security Council than could be provided by the intergovernmental sanctions committee.[49]

The passage of UNSC Resolution 1874 in June and the ongoing efforts on the part of the United States to enforce it was again met by

Table 5. Interdiction of Shipments in Relation to Sanctions against North Korea					
Date	Country of interdiction	Goods	Departure Country	Destination Country	Comment
Dec 2007	Austria	3 Steinway concert pianos	Austria	North Korea	
Oct and Dec 2008	Japan	luxury goods, i.e., 34 pianos, 4 Mercedes-Benz automobiles, and cosmetics	Japan	North Korea	
Jan 2009	Democratic People's Republic of Congo	arms and ammunition	allegedly North Korea	Democratic People's Republic of Congo	North Korean vessel *Birobong*
May 2009	Italy	2 luxury yachts	Italy	North Korea	
Jul 2009	United Arab Emirates	10 containers of munitions, detonators, explosives, and rocket-propelled grenades	North Korea	Iran	Vessel owned by an Australian subsidiary of a French company under a Bahamian flag; trans-shipped several times
Jul 2009	Italy	high-end electrical/electronic apparatus for recording and reproducing sound and images	Italy	North Korea	
Aug 2009	Italy	150 bottles of cognac, 270 bottles of whiskey	Italy	North Korea	
Sept 2009	South Korea	chemical safety suits (dual use: military utility for chemical protection)	North Korea	allegedly Syria	Panama vessel MSC *Rachele*; Syria denies being destination; trans-shipped in China
Dec 2009	Thailand	35 tons of arms, including parts of long-range missile Daepodong #2	North Korea	allegedly Iran	Georgian cargo plane; Iran denies being destination
Nov 2009	South Africa	tank parts (Soviet-designed T-54 and T-55 tanks)	North Korea	Congo-Brazzaville (Republic of Congo)	French cargo vessel; trans-shipped in China and Malaysia

Source: United Nations Security Council 2010.
Note: In June of 2009, a North Korean vessel named *Kang-nam 1*, allegedly on its way to Myanmar, was tracked by US Navy vessels for weeks on suspicion of carrying illegal weapons. Inspection was not carried out, however, and the ship turned around and returned to Nampo Port in North Korea.

North Korean escalation. In June, the Foreign Ministry announced that the country would weaponize all newly extracted plutonium,[50] commence a uranium enrichment (HEU) program, and provide a "decisive military response" to any "blockade" against the country. According to the statement, it had "become an absolutely impossible option for the DPRK to even think about giving up its nuclear weapons."

Yet, at the same time that North Korea was escalating, it also began to signal a willingness to reengage, raising the question of whether the sanctions had had effect.[51] The crucial issue—and one that continued to plague the negotiations through the end of 2010—concerned the format under which any negotiations would take place. The United States repeatedly stated its willingness to engage with North Korea, including bilaterally, as long as those talks were held "within the framework" of the Six Party Talks process.[52] The reason for insisting on this format was both procedural and substantive. Not only did it provide a multilateral venue for coordinating with Japan, South Korea, China, and Russia, but holding negotiations under the aegis of the Six Party Talks assured that their central focus would be on the process of denuclearization. In urging North Korea's return to the Six Party Talks process, the United States also repeatedly stated that it was opposed to "talks for talks' sake," which appeared to suggest that it was imposing preconditions on the talks. In particular, the United States sought to reconfirm Pyongyang's commitment to agreements made in prior rounds of the talks, most notably in the September 2005 statement of principles and the implementation accords of February and October 2007.

> *The US repeatedly stated that it was opposed to "talks for talks' sake"*

At the same time that it invited a return to the Six Party Talks, the Obama administration also made clear that no further inducements would be offered to North Korea in advance of returning to the talks, including the relaxation of sanctions. In a widely cited comment at the ASEAN Regional Forum in Singapore in May 2009, Secretary of Defense Robert Gates said the United States was "tired of buying the same horse twice," and expressed opposition to "the notion that we buy our way back to the status quo ante." The United States also argued (and rightly from a legal point of view) that it was not in a position to relax

Engaging North Korea: The Role of Economic Statecraft 57

multilateral sanctions; any such change would be contingent on North Korea taking the actions called for under the UN Security Council resolutions.

Yet if the United States was unwilling to offer inducements for the purpose of getting North Korea back to the talks, the question remained of what *prospective* benefits it might offer. The administration was unwilling to commit to *finalizing* the process of normalization prior to complete denuclearization, and for good political reasons; it seemed implausible that such a process could even begin, let alone reach a conclusion, while North Korea remained a de facto nuclear power. However, the United States also recognized clearly, in the words of a senior official, that "if North Korea is to take major steps to dismantle its nuclear capabilities that there must be a corresponding set of initiatives on the part of not only the United States but South Korea, China, and Japan."[53] Given the difficulties of implementing all components of the agenda outlined in the September 2005 statement of principles at one time, it seemed inevitable that the talks would focus on the phasing of concessions—for example, by holding negotiations on denuclearization in tandem with discussions about a peace regime and normalization and by phasing inducements and reciprocal actions.

North Korean policy showed less coherence during 2009–2010 than it did under the Bush administration, when the regime showed surprising consistency in its core demands of security assurances, normalization, and economic assistance in return for commitments to denuclearization. North Korean statements in 2009 and 2010 appeared more erratic—for example, suggesting that it sought an end to the nuclear umbrella or even de jure recognition as a nuclear weapons state. However, over the course of late 2009, a more coherent North Korean strategy emerged that was deeply at odds not only with US views, but with the view of the other five parties with respect to the Six Party Talks.

North Korea appeared to support a return to multilateral talks, and to accept the ultimate objective of denuclearization. The brief mention of foreign policy issues in the 2010 New Year's editorial—the regime's major policy statement for each year—is typical of these statements:

The fundamental problem arising in guaranteeing the peace and stability of the Korean peninsula and the region today is putting an end to the hostile relationship between the DPRK and the

United States. Our position to provide a solid peace regime on the Korean peninsula and realize denuclearization through dialogue and negotiations remains consistent. (KCNA 2010)

However, more elaborated North Korean proposals revealed that the significance of this statement was to be found in its ordering of the issues. According to North Korean statements, the fundamental problem was ultimately a bilateral one. Resolving that hostility through multilateral talks among the armistice parties and bilateral talks with the United States was a precondition for even resuming—let alone completing—the agenda spelled out through the Six Party Talks process. Indeed, North Korea's statements appear calculated to signal a commitment to negotiations, while casting doubt on the utility and even legitimacy of the Six Party Talks. In an early formulation of the proposal by the Foreign Ministry, for example, North Korea allows that talks on a peace regime may be held "either at a separate forum as laid down in the September 19 Joint Statement or in the framework of the six-party talks for the denuclearization of the Korean Peninsula like the DPRK-US talks now under way in view of their nature and significance."[54] It even goes so far as to acknowledge US statements that it lacked hostile intent toward North Korea. But at the same time, the statement makes clear that the peace regime and bilateral talks, and the associated lifting of sanctions, are a precondition for addressing the agenda of the Six Party Talks.[55]

These differences appear similar to the procedural difficulties the Bush administration faced in 2003, when it refused to talk directly to the North Koreans. China again sought to bridge the divide through intense diplomatic activity in February and March of 2010. These initiatives were built around a procedural proposal that would grant North Korea much-sought bilateral meetings with the United States, but would be followed by a preparatory six-party meeting in anticipation of a full resumption of the Six Party Talks. But the problems were not merely ones of venue, but also of the commitments that were assumed. Accepting the Chinese proposal, the United States saw the steps as linked, with the bilateral meetings tied to a commitment to resume the talks. Despite early Chinese optimism about the proposal, North Korea remained silent on it, apparently continuing to insist on its own preconditions in the form of a lifting of sanctions, bilateral talks, and peace regime negotiations. Before these proposals could come to fruition, the *Cheonan* incident occurred.

From the *Cheonan* to the Shelling of Yeonpyeong Island

The sinking of the *Cheonan* marked the culmination of a steady escalation of North-South tensions following the inauguration of Lee Myung-bak in February 2008. The Lee administration explicitly rejected the engagement strategy of the Kim Dae-jung and Roh Moo-hyun governments, and argued that economic, and even humanitarian, inducements to North Korea should be conditional on progress concerning the nuclear question. Pyongyang's response to this change of course was generally escalatory, even vitriolic. Virtually all aspects of North-South relations were adversely affected, from the elaborate structure of North-South meetings built up over the previous decade to trade, aid, and investment (Figure 7).[56]

Military escalation between North and South centered not on the demilitarized zone (DMZ), but on the de facto maritime border in the Yellow Sea, the so-called Northern Limit Line (NLL).[57] In 2007, the North-South summit between outgoing president Roh Moo-hyun and Kim Jong-il proposed that the two sides negotiate a "peace zone" in the Yellow Sea that would replace the NLL. Although this confidence-building measure faced severe political constraints in South Korea even under the Roh administration, Lee Myung-bak explicitly backed away from the "peace zone" proposals.

> *Military escalation between North and South centered not on the DMZ, but on the maritime border*

In early 2009, as North Korea was signaling its intention to undertake a long-range missile test, it also began a sustained escalation around the NLL.[58] In January 2009, Pyongyang declared its intention to protect its own alternative version of the maritime border and suggested it would not be bound by the armistice. Tensions around the issue escalated further when South Korea joined the Proliferation Security Initiative (PSI) in the wake of the second nuclear test in May 2009. The North Korean military responded by declaring that any actions under the PSI would be considered an act of war, and that it could not guarantee the "legal status" of five South Korean islands that the NLL had been drawn to incorporate. Throughout the remainder of the year and into early 2010, North Korea repeatedly conducted short-range missile and artillery tests off both coasts. Following a North Korean incursion on November 9, the two navies engaged in a confrontation that resulted in the damage of a North Korean vessel and loss of life; this event was widely viewed as an important precursor to the subsequent sinking of the *Cheonan* the following March.

The question of how the Lee Myung-bak government handled the investigation of the *Cheonan*, whether it was used for political purposes, and whether the North Koreans were even culpable, became charged political questions in South Korea. The most important consequence, however, was the effect of the South Korean response on US strategies toward North Korea.

The joint investigative committee made its first announcement with respect to the incident on May 20. Without releasing a full report, it claimed that a North Korean torpedo attack was responsible for the sinking of *Cheonan*. In a nationally televised address from the Korean War Memorial on May 24, President Lee announced a number of actions against the North, including a suspension of trade and exchanges, a ban on the ability of the North's merchant ships to transit South Korean waters, and plans to install loudspeakers along the DMZ to resume psychological warfare. Subsequently, the Lee administration held that the Six Party Talks could not resume until North Korea issued an apology with respect to the *Cheonan*, although the administration was later constrained to back away from that position.

Even before the full report of the incident had been made public, Secretary of State Clinton endorsed the Lee administration's approach, including its intention to bring the issue before the UN Security Council, and hinted at a full review of all US policies toward North Korea.[59] Over the next several months, the United States sent a number of further signals to North Korea, including military ones. In July, the administration announced its intention to conduct naval exercises off both coasts and moved to delay the transfer of wartime operational control of Korean forces from the Combined Forces Command back to the South Korean military.

In a highly symbolic press conference at the DMZ in July, Secretary of State Clinton—accompanied by Secretary of Defense Gates—announced the administration's intention to levy new sanctions on

North Korea as well. Less than a month later, President Barack Obama signed a new executive order targeting any entity that facilitates North Korean arms trafficking, the import of luxury foods, or any other illicit activity on behalf of Pyongyang, including money laundering, counterfeiting of goods and currency, and cash smuggling. Whereas existing authority had focused on entities involved in WMD-related materials and the missile program, the new authority allowed the United States to target entities involved in the trade of luxury items, as well as conventional arms exports. In addition, the US Treasury and State departments announced expanded sanctions against five entities found to be in violation of the existing Executive Order 13382, aimed at freezing the assets of those engaged in WMD proliferation.[60] In announcing the new sanctions, Robert Einhorn, a full-time sanctions "czar" with responsibilities for both Iran and North Korea, stated specifically that although the United States held open the offer to resume talks, it was not prepared to reward North Korea simply for returning to the negotiating table.

> *Obama signed a new executive order targeting arms trafficking and luxury items to North Korea*

The North Koreans again responded to sanctions by escalating. After American scientist Siegfried Hecker visited Yongbyon at North Korea's invitation, he reported on November 20, 2010, that he had witnessed an estimated 1,000 centrifuges in operation at the nuclear complex. Hecker's revelation implied a significant intelligence failure among US and allied governments, raised questions about the extent of North Korean cooperation with third parties such as Iran and Pakistan, and revealed effective North Korean circumvention of UNSC Resolutions 1718 and 1874.

Only a few days later, on November 23, 2010, North Korea shelled Yeonpyeong Island near the disputed Northern Limit Line (NLL), killing two South Korean military personnel and two South Korean civilians, injuring an additional score, and devastating the island's infrastructure. The stated justification was the ongoing North Korean rejection of the legitimacy of the NLL and the threats posed by joint US–South Korean military exercises in its vicinity.

Even more clearly than in the past, China's actions suggested an extreme unwillingness to take sides against North Korea. After issuing bland calls for calm "on both sides," and blocking UN Security Council action on the matter,[61] China called for an "emergency session" of the Six Party Talks. By this time, however, the prospects for diplomacy had evaporated, and policy had shifted from economic constraints toward more direct efforts to signal the credibility of the military deterrent. The Chinese proposal was quickly rejected by South Korea, the United States, and Japan. Instead, the United States and South Korea went forward with planned joint naval exercises in the Yellow Sea involving the US aircraft carrier *George Washington*, despite earlier Chinese objections. President Lee Myung-bak replaced the defense minister, and both he and the new defense minister made public comments about more forceful military responses to future North Korean provocations. In addition, South Korea undertook the largest civil defense drill in decades. US Chairman of the Joint Chiefs of Staff Adm. Mike Mullen reenforced this message by visiting Seoul and signaling support for a marked relaxation of South Korean rules of engagement.

> *China called for an emergency session of the talks, but the prospects for diplomacy had evaporated*

By the end of 2010, these measures had not had the effect of eliciting North Korean concessions, again sparking debate about the appropriate course of action. In both the United States and South Korea, a minority argued that the two allies were caught in the same dynamic as the Bush administration, with sanctions only serving to escalate rather than mitigate tensions, and with some form of engagement providing the only way out.[62]

However, the ultimate policy response in both countries rested on political developments that appeared to move away from rather than toward engagement. Public opinion in South Korea swung strongly behind the Lee administration. President Lee outlined an unapologetic defense of the strategy of reciprocity and further tightened economic sanctions, leaving Kaesong as the only point of economic contact between North and South. In the United States, the November 2010 congressional elections resulted in a Republican majority in the US House of Representatives and a narrowed Democratic majority in the

Senate. The implications of this tectonic political shift on American foreign policy remain unclear as of this writing, but they certainly suggest a reduced capacity of the administration to make concessions. The current situation is potentially reminiscent of the difficulties the Clinton administration faced after Republicans took control of Congress in 1994 and proceeded to use North Korea policy as a cudgel to beat the Clinton administration (Noland 2000, Hathaway and Tama 2004). Although a deepening food crisis in early 2011 provided an opportunity for a humanitarian gesture, the Obama administration faced a variety of Republican concerns with respect to North Korea, from working conditions in Kaesong and human rights problems to the lack of progress on denuclearization through the Six Party Talks process.

Conclusion

Three points emerge from this analysis. The first has to do with domestic politics in North Korea, including both its capacity to absorb pressure and its interest in engagement. The extraordinary repressiveness of the regime clearly calls into question the utility of broad commercial sanctions against North Korea, assuming they could even be coordinated. There is some evidence that financial sanctions had an *economic* effect in both 2006 and again after 2009; by early 2011, the country was experiencing a steadily worsening food crisis and had pressed foreign capitals, the World Food Program, and nongovernmental organizations (NGOs) for assistance. Nonetheless, sanctions did not deter the regime from testing its first nuclear device, sinking the *Cheonan*, or shelling Yeonpyeong Island, Nor, as of this writing, did sanctions lead to the long-awaited "strategic shift" or to signals from North Korea that it was willing to resume the Six Party Talks without simultaneous bilateral talks and peace regime negotiations.

Indeed, evidence on North Korean intent to engage is elusive. The evidence considered on domestic political developments is consistent with an interpretation that North Korean intentions were not constant over time. When the Bush administration came to office, North Korea was in a relatively reformist phase; this opening was almost completely missed by the Bush administration, which was preoccupied with intelligence on the country's HEU program and highly skeptical of North Korean intentions. Over time, however, the mixed results of the reforms and the worsening external environment led to clear shifts in economic policy that are suggestive of deeper political changes in the regime. Particularly after 2005, and culminating with the disastrous currency reform of 2009, "military first" had taken a much harder form. Resource allocation tilted toward military priorities, and the market was viewed with increasing skepticism.

From August 2008, Kim Jong-il's likely stroke and the onset of the succession process compounded the problems. These domestic political events coincided with a further "hardening" of the regime around core bases of support, a preoccupation with showing resolve, and a declining willingness to make tradeoffs. In combination, these domestic political shifts may help explain the particularly unwelcoming stance North Korea took toward the incoming Obama administration, a stance that deeply colored Washington's reaction to the missile and nuclear tests of 2009.

North Korea's unwelcoming stance deeply colored Washington's reaction to the 2009 missile and nuclear tests

A second conclusion is that the efforts of the Bush administration to pressure North Korea were consistently undermined by severe coordination problems. South Korea pursued a strategy of relatively unconditional engagement through 2007, and even Japan sought normalization until its policy was hijacked by the abductee issue. But China's role was clearly pivotal. China has been consistent in its rhetorical commitment to denuclearization. Beijing has played a key role in brokering the talks, offered crucial inducements to keep the talks going, and even signaled its displeasure through support of multilateral statements and sanctions, particularly in 2009. But it has been consistently unwilling to use its vast commercial and aid leverage to force a reckoning. To the contrary, North Korea's foreign economic relations have become more rather than less dependent on China, compounding the diplomatic difficulties of bringing pressure to bear on the country.

This conclusion gains force through a consideration of the North Korean response to pressure and sanctions. There is little evidence from our narrative that ratcheting up pressure "worked"; to the contrary, it generated escalatory responses and served to poison negotiations. To the extent that it did work, it did so through a diplomatic process that spelled out for North Korea the benefits of compliance with its international obligations, as well as the costs of not doing so. Sanctions can be justified on purely defensive grounds: as a means of limiting North Korea's WMD or proliferation activity. But as a tactical tool to induce concessions at the bargaining table, the track record is more limited.

But inducements have posed difficulties as well. Inducements have periodically worked to restart talks—for example, in the round of talks in 2005 that led to the September joint statement. There is also some limited evidence that very tightly calibrated reciprocal actions worked in 2008 before being politically derailed. But inducements "worked" only with respect to one component, albeit an important one, of the problem at hand: the production of fissile material at Yongbyon. Addressing this issue effectively would have been a worthy achievement, and might have provided the springboard for the so-called "third phase" of negotiations. A gradual lessening of mistrust might have produced a more timely implementation of commitments and avoided the overt military actions of 2009–10.

But even if Yongbyon were disabled, a daunting agenda would have remained: an effective return to the NPT and IAEA inspections, proliferation, missiles, existing stockpiles of fissile material, and the weapons themselves. Compared to the production of plutonium, uranium enrichment would have posed particularly difficult inspection and verification issues, as subsequently learned from the stunning revelations of the extent of the country's HEU program in late 2010. Moreover, there was strong evidence that the North Koreans were unwilling to address important aspects of this remaining agenda, including proliferation and HEU in particular. With changing political dynamics in North Korea and the cushion provided by its external economic relations with China, such a bargaining process would have effectively acknowledged a nuclear North Korea for some time.

What implications might our conclusions have for our understanding of other cases, including the successful denuclearization of Libya and the ongoing challenges posed by Iran? A first point is the ongoing significance of coordination problems. Libya has been advanced as a case demonstrating how diplomacy and inducements can "work" (Jentleson and Whytock 2005–2006). But at the time, Libya lacked the enabling supporters that North Korea and Iran have been able to rely on, notably China and, in Iran's case, Russia as well.

The role of oil is also double-edged in this regard. A frequently made argument by North Korea watchers is that Libya's denuclearization was facilitated by its status as an oil exporter. With alternative sources of energy and foreign exchange, it was less costly for Libya to abandon its nuclear program than it would be for North Korea. But a valuable exportable commodity such as oil can frustrate denuclearization by impeding the formation of sanctioning coalitions; Iran demonstrates this problem clearly.

The security context—at least as read by the target state—is also significant. With the March 2011 imposition of a no-fly zone over Libya, the lessons that Pyongyang draws from the Libyan experience could be exactly the opposite of what the US government would like to convey.[63] North Korea has repeatedly stated that it sees nuclear weapons as a legitimate deterrent against a "hostile policy." Iran has clearly used nuclear weapons to its strategic advantage. The North Korean leadership could well conclude that despite whatever assurances the United States and its allies might offer, the maintenance of a nuclear capability is necessary to avoid the foreign military intervention that occurred in Iraq and Libya. The announcement that International Criminal Court (ICC) prosecutor Luis Moreno-Ocampo is opening a human rights investigation into Libya's Colonel Gaddafi, three of his sons, and four of his aides underlines that the issue goes to regime survival in the most personal sense. In December, following the sinking of the *Cheonan* and the shelling of Yeonpyeong Island, the ICC launched a similar war crimes investigation aimed at the Kim regime.[64]

The lesson Pyongyang derives from Libya could be the opposite of what the US wishes

Thus, the story comes full circle: North Korea's political economy and its external relations render it remarkably insensitive to either sanctions or inducements. Instead, its behavior appears driven to a significant extent by domestic political considerations and a preoccupation with regime survival. It is conceivable that as the regime consolidates power internally, it may be more willing to undertake risks and engage in negotiations more seriously and substantively than it has to date. And it is at least possible that external constraints have simply not imposed enough pain, and that the country's worsening food shortages might push the regime to reengage or to exploit a humanitarian gesture.

But the converse appears equally, if not more, plausible. The post–Kim Jong-il leadership will prove too politically insecure or divided to make meaningful concessions, and the gradual consolidation of power will only reinforce the preexisting trends toward a more hard-line and truculent policy. If so, the ultimate resolution of the North Korean nuclear issue may await fundamental change in the political regime.

Appendix 1:
Trade Data Selection

Data on North Korean trade flows is available from the Korea Trade-Investment Promotion Agency (KOTRA), the IMF's Direction of Trade Statistics (DOTS), and the United Nations Commodity Trade Statistics Database (COMTRADE). KOTRA and DOTS provide data on North Korea's overall merchandise trade balance and a bilateral breakdown of North Korean trade, and mirror statistics from COMTRADE make available the commodity composition of North Korean trade as reported by the country's trading partners. North Korea's trade data as reported by these three sources in many cases is not in agreement, with discrepancies arising from different reporting practices, country selection, and the inclusion of potentially erroneously reported data in both DOTS and COMTRADE.

Discrepancies due to differences in reporting practices and data cleaning procedures emerge in a comparison of North Korea's bilateral trade data as reported in KOTRA and DOTS, where sufficient country overlap can be found. KOTRA, for example, removes merchandise trade arising from bilateral aid transfers, while DOTS leaves bilateral aid in the merchandise trade series, as valued by the donor country. The most pronounced example of this source of discrepancy between the two datasets shows up in reported imports from Japan in 2001, where North Korean imports from Japan jump to US$1,169 million in 2001, up from $225 million in 2000. In 2002, this number drops to $146 million and steadily declines thereafter. Alternatively, KOTRA reports that North Korean merchandise imports from Japan totaled US$249 million in 2001, $920 million dollars less than the level of imports reported by DOTS. Looking at the commodity composition of Japanese exports to North Korea in 2001 in COMTRADE, it becomes apparent that the source of this discrepancy comes from approximately US$1 billion in rice[65] shipped from Japan—presumably in the form of food aid—that was likely either stripped from the KOTRA series or repriced by KOTRA.[66]

A second source of discrepancy between KOTRA and DOTS trade data for North Korea comes from country selection; there are many countries that are included in the DOTS trade series that have been omitted from the KOTRA series and vice versa. Country selection does appear to account for a substantial share of the difference between KOTRA and DOTS trade totals for years in which bilateral trade data is available for both sources.[67]

It may be the case that, for certain countries, customs officials are mixing up North and South Korea in the trade data they ultimately report to the UN. While it is difficult to prove this from the point of view of imports into North Korea, what these countries report as importing from North Korea can be more revealing. According to COMTRADE, Brazil, for example, reports a dramatic increase in imports from North Korea between the mid-1990s up through the present, the composition of which appears to be much like that of South Korea's. Forty-two percent of Brazil's reported imports over the period 1990–2006 are classified as machinery and transport equipment, including office machines, telecommunications equipment, and other electrical machinery. Such a suspect commodity composition of exports may help to explain why bilateral trade data between the North and Brazil appears to have been omitted from the KOTRA series, and also explains why it is not included in this exercise. Other notable examples of questionable reporting of imports from North Korea include Ghana, Costa Rica, Guatemala, and Honduras, all of which report large amount of imports of either telecommunications equipment, household appliances, automobiles, automobile parts, and other types of complex manufactures that closely track the commodity composition of South Korean exports.

Based on these and other similar observations, KOTRA's data on North Korean commercial merchandise trade seems more plausible than the alternatives. This is not to claim that the KOTRA trade data is flawless; it is likely that some countries that should have been included were omitted, and therefore KOTRA's trade data likely understates, to some small degree, North Korea's overall level of trade. It is likely, however, that the North's net trade position in goods is fairly accurate, especially when taken in comparison to other more uncertain transactions that recorded in the North Korean balance of payments. In determining and analyzing North Korea's external position, KOTRA's data provides the most accurate insights into trade in goods. This paper utilized KOTRA data for trade between North and South Korea, and for recent trade figures (2004–2008), it extensively compared KOTRA and DOTS figures to recreate a more comprehensive and reasonable trade dataset for North Korea.

Appendix 2:
Data Sources and Methods

Sample period: 2001q3 – 2010q2.

Total Exports: Monthly export data (Chinese exports to North Korea) was summed to generate quarterly exports.
Source: KITA (Korean International Trade Association) and General Administration of Customs, People's Republic of China (PRC).

Cereal Exports (price adjusted): Exports of HS (Harmonized System) two-digit code10 (cereals) were used for this variable.[68] Due to the volatility of cereal prices in recent years (Figure A), data was price adjusted. Four main cereals—wheat, barley, maize, and rice—made up more than 97 percent of Chinese cereal exports to North Korea each year between 2000 and 2009. UN COMTRADE's annual export data of these four commodities (2000–2009) was used to calculate the weight of each commodity in Chinese cereal exports to North Korea, and these weights were applied to the monthly IMF commodity price data to calculate the final price index (wheat, US No.1 HRW, fob Gulf of Mexico; barley, Canadian Western No. 1 Spot; maize; US No. 2 yellow, fob Gulf of Mexico; rice, 5 percent broken, nominal price quote, fob Bangkok).

By dividing each monthly price index by the price index of the first observation, the conversion factor was then calculated (e.g., 2000M1=1, 2010M6=0.56). By multiplying this conversion factor to the Chinese cereal export data (to North Korea), price-adjusted cereal export data is retrieved.

Sources: KITA (Korea International Trade Association), citing General Administration of Customs, PRC. IMF (International Monetary Fund), available at: http://www.imf.org/external/np/res/commod/index.asp

Appendix 2 Figure A. Price-adjusted Chinese Cereal Exports to North Korea

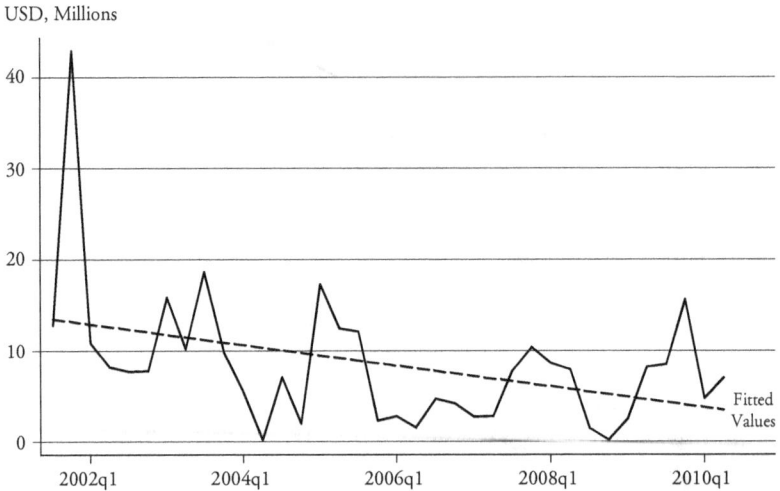

USD, Millions

Fuel Exports (price adjusted): Exports of HS 27 (mineral fuels, mineral oils, bituminous substances, mineral waxes) was used. Similarly, fuel prices faced substantial volatility in recent years (Figure B), and therefore the export data was price adjusted. Coal and petroleum made up on average 97 percent of total Chinese fuel exports to North Korea, making possible the application of the prices of these two commodities to calculate the fuel price index. UN COMTRADE's annual export data for coal and petroleum was used to calculate the weight of each commodity in Chinese fuel exports to North Korea, and then these weights were applied to the monthly commodity price data to calculate the final price index for fuel exports. (Coal, coal thermal for export, Australia; petroleum, average Petroleum Spot index of UK Brent, Dubai, and West Texas.) By dividing each monthly price index by the price index of the first observation, the conversion factor was calculated, and by multiplying this conversion factor to the Chinese fuel export data (to North Korea), price-adjusted fuel export data is retrieved.

Sources: KITA (Korea International Trade Association), citing General Administration of Customs, PRC. International Monetary Fund, available at: http://www.imf.org/external/np/res/commod/index.asp

Appendix 2 Figure B. Price-adjusted Chinese Fuel Exports to North Korea

USD, Millions

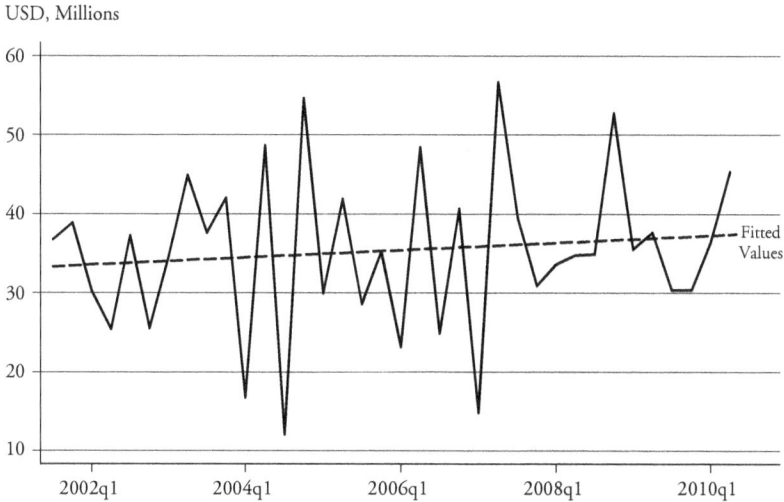

North Korea's GDP: Annual real GDP presented in South Korean won (2000–2009) from the Bank of Korea was used. For the geometric interpolation (temporal disaggregation from annual data to quarterly data), cubic spline interpolation was used. Annual GDP data divided by four was used for the mid-year value for each year, and interpolation was done for the rest of the period. Extrapolation was done for 2010 mid-year value. This was indexed so that the initial observation 2000q1=100 was logged.
Source: Bank of Korea, available at: ecos.bok.or.kr.

North Korea's Exchange Rates (Price Proxy): North Korean won (NKW)/Chinese renminbi (RMB) exchange rate data are incomplete, especially in the earlier sample period. Implied RMB and USD exchange rates, in terms of relative NKW prices, tend to be very close to actual RMB/USD rates, and therefore used the NKW/USD exchange rates to determine both RMB (where NKW/RMB data are not available). Since there were months where neither the NKW/RMB nor the NKW/USD data are available, interpolation at the monthly level was carried out for certain months. This exchange rate was then inversed to RMB/NKW exchange rate and was logged after being collapsed into quarterly data. See Noland 2009b for an explanation of the economic theory behind the inclusion of this variable.

Source: Good Friends, *North Korea Today,* various issues; *NK In & Out,* various issues; Daily NK, various issues; *Open Radio for North Korea,* various issues; Institute for Far Eastern Studies—Kyungnam University's *NK Brief,* various issues; IMF's *International Financial Statistics (IFS).*

Nuclear Sanctions: UN Resolution 1718 went into effect in October 2006. This dummy variable is equal to zero from the beginning of the sample through the third quarter of 2006, and equal to one from the fourth quarter of 2006 through the end of the sample. UN Resolution 1874 went into effect in June 2009. This dummy variable is equal to zero from the beginning of the sample through the second quarter of 2009, and equal to one from the third quarter of 2009 through the end of the sample.

Appendix 3:
Heavy Oil Shipments to North Korea, 2007–2009

One issue of debate is whether the five parties fulfilled their obligations to supply North Korea with the HFO commitments under the February and October roadmap agreements, which totaled 1 million MT divided equally among the five. The agreements allowed for the delivery of either HFO or "HFO equivalents." Table A shows total energy assistance over the period. Japan refused to provide HFO support until North Korea had adequately addressed the issue of abductees. Table B shows estimates by Manyin and Nikitin of the timing of the 450,000 MT of total shipments through December 2008, which reflects both ongoing conflicts over the terms of North Korean compliance and

Appendix 3 Table A. Energy Assistance to North Korea July 2007–March 2009			
	HFO delivered (MT)	HFO equivalent delivered (MT)	Undelivered
China	50,000	150,000	0
Japan	0	0	200,000
Russia	200,000	0	0
South Korea	50,000	95,110	54,890 equivalent
United States	200,000	0	0
Total	500,000	245,110	254,890

political and logistical constraints in the donor countries (Manyin and Nikitin 2010 and communication with the authors). After the United States stated that further shipments would not be forthcoming, China and Russia sought to keep the agreement alive by fulfilling its obligations, but without success.

Appendix 3 Table B. Timing of Heavy Oil Shipments July 2007–December 2008

Shipment date	Donor	Amount delivered (MT)
July 2007	South Korea	50,000
September 2007	China	50,000
November 2007	US	46,000
January 2008	Russia	50,000
March 2008	US	54,000
May 2008	Russia	50,000
July 2008	US	34,000
August 2008	US	16,000
November 2008	US	50,000
December 2008	Russia	50,000
Total		450,000

Appendix 4:
Economic Sanctions Currently Imposed on North Korea in Furtherance of US Foreign Policy or National Security Objectives

Statutory Basis [regulation]		Rationale	Restriction
Export Administration Act of 1979		General foreign policy reasons	Limits the export of goods or services
	Sec. 5	National security controls, Communism	Limits the export of goods or services
	Sec. 5(b)	Communism	Limits the export of goods or services
	Sec. 11B	Proliferation of weapons of mass destruction: missiles	Prohibits a range of transactions—contracts, export licenses, imports into US
Foreign Assistance Act of 1961	Sec. 307	General foreign policy reasons	Limits proportionate share to international organizations which, in turn, expend funds in North Korea
	Sec. 620(t)	Diplomatic relations severed	Prohibits most foreign aid and agricultural sales under P.L. 480
	Sec. 620(f)	Communism	Prohibits foreign aid
Department of Defense Appropriations Act, 2010		General foreign policy reasons	Prohibits assistance from defense appropriations
Department of State, Foreign Operations, and Related Programs Appropriations Act		General foreign policy reasons	Prohibits bilateral assistance
	Sec. 7071(f)	Proliferation of weapons of mass destruction: nuclear detonations	Prohibits Economic Support Funds for energy-related programs
	Title VI	Proliferation of weapons of mass destruction: nuclear detonations	Prohibits Export-Import Bank financing
Export-Import Bank Act of 1945	Sec. 2(b)(2)	Communism	Prohibits Export-Import Bank funding to Marxist-Leninist states
	Sec. 2(b)(4)	Proliferation of weapons of mass destruction: nuclear detonations	Prohibits Export-Import Bank financing

Statutory Basis [regulation]		Rationale	Restriction
Bretton Woods Agreements Act	Sec. 43	Communism	Prohibits support in the IFIs
Trade Act of 1974	Sec. 401	Communism	Denies favorable trade terms
	Sec. 402	Nonmarket economy and emigration	Denies favorable trade terms
	Sec. 409	Nonmarket economy and emigration	Denies favorable trade terms
	Sec. 406	Communism and market disruption	Denies favorable trade terms
State Department Basic Authorities Act	Sec. 205	Communism	Prohibits the acquisition of property in US for diplomatic mission
Arms Export Control Act	Sec. 40A	Terrorism, failure to cooperate with US efforts	Prohibits transactions related to defense articles and defense services
	Sec. 73	Proliferation of weapons of mass destruction: missiles	Prohibits a range of transactions—US Government contracts, export licenses, imports into United States
	Sec. 101	Proliferation of weapons of mass destruction: nuclear enrichment transfers	Prohibits foreign aid, military aid
	Sec. 102	Proliferation of weapons of mass destruction: nuclear reprocessing transfers, nuclear detonations	Prohibits foreign aid (except humanitarian), military aid, USG defense sales and transfers, export licenses for USML goods and services, US Government-backed credits, support in the international banks, agricultural credits or financing, US commercial bank financing, licenses for export of certain goods and services
Miscellaneous Appropriations, 2000	Sec. 501	Excessive military expenditure, human rights violations	Prohibits the cancellation or reduction of certain debt
International Emergency Economic Powers Act & National Emergencies Act		National emergency, proliferation of weapons of mass destruction	Blocks assets of named proliferators of weapons of mass destruction
		National emergency	Prohibits imports, exports, transactions related to transportation
		National emergency, proliferation of weapons of mass destruction, attack of the *Cheonan*, nuclear detonations, missile launches, violation of UNSCR resolutions, counterfeiting of goods and currency, money laundering, smuggling, narcotics trafficking, destabilizing the region	Blocks assets of, and transactions with or on behalf of, named entities

Statutory Basis [regulation]		Rationale	Restriction
Iran, North Korea, and Syria Non-proliferation Act of 2000	Sec. 3	Proliferation of weapons of mass destruction	Prohibits a range of transactions —arms sales and exports, dual-use exports, procurement contracts, assistance, imports, support in the international banks, credit, landing rights
Trafficking Victims Protection Act of 2000	Sec. 10	Human rights (trafficking in persons)	Prohibits non-humanitarian foreign aid, cultural exchanges, support in international financial institutions
31 USC 5318A (referred to by its amendatory vehicle - Sec. 311, USA PATRIOT Act)		Counterfeiting, money-laundering	Prohibits certain commercial bank transactions
Derived from Rennack 2010.			

Endnotes

1. In addition to a five-megawatt electric (MWe) research reactor, the facility also housed a fuel rod fabrication plant and a reprocessing facility, disingenuously called a radiochemistry laboratory. This facility was the source of the fissile material ultimately used in the 2006 and 2009 nuclear tests.

2. Formally, the Joint Statement of the Fourth Round of the Six Party Talks, Beijing, September 19, 2005.

3. The participants in the Six Party Talks include the two Koreas, China, Japan, Russia, and the United States. References to "the five parties" are to the six minus North Korea.

4. We define "engagement" to mean both a willingness to negotiate—literally, to engage—as well as to consider positive inducements, including but not limited to economic ones. Noneconomic inducements relevant in the Korean context include normalization of diplomatic relations and security guarantees. Economic inducements include the lifting of sanctions and the provision of various forms of economic assistance, including entry into international financial institutions.

5. This is the central reason why Milner and Kubota (2005) argue that democracies have more open trade regimes than autocracies.

6. The most comprehensive treatment of the repressive apparatus can be found in the Korean Institute for National Unification (KINU) *White Paper on Human Rights in North Korea*.

7. The concept of "military first politics" was not unveiled until later in the decade, but evidence of a close reliance on the military was visible well before then. At the time of his father's death, the three most significant positions held by Kim Jong-il were the chairmanship of the National Defense Commission (NDC), his position as commander-in-chief of the Korean People's Army (KPA), and his effective control of the Organization and Guidance Department of the party, responsible for all personnel matters. During the interregnum, he ruled through ad hoc structures consisting of all or selected members of the politburo and those military and security apparatus leaders who belonged to either or both of the Workers' Party of

Korea (KWP) Central Military Affairs Committee and the NDC. See Koh 2005 for an excellent summary of the rollout of the *songun* concept.

8. As the chairman of the Supreme People's Assembly stated in his nomination speech: "The National Defense Commission chairman's position is the highest state position that protects the socialist fatherland state institutions and the people's destiny, and organizes and directs the activities for strengthening and developing the state's defense and overall national capabilities by commanding the state's political, economic, and military capabilities in their entirety." (Yonhap News Agency 2003, 113–114).

9. The anti-market campaigns began with the imposition of escalating age restrictions on market traders in the fall of 2007, and were followed by stepped-up inspections of the general markets and a dramatic reduction in their days of operation.

10. One recent development, a crackdown on the use of privately owned vehicles, is not reassuring in this regard (Institute for Far Eastern Studies, 2010b). At the same time, the regime permitted the expanded use of cell phones, with Egyptian cellular provider Orascom claiming that it had extended service to 75 percent of the country and signed up more than 300,000 subscribers (Associated Press, "Orascom Telecom Sees Surge in North Korea Subscribers," November 8, 2010). The crackdown on private economic activity and the acquiescence of private cell phone use can be reconciled if phone use is confined to the politically loyal. Still, the regime's apparently relaxed attitude toward private communications technology is striking.

11. According to a Congressional Research Service (CRS) memorandum, China's opposition prevented the United Nations Security Council (UNSC) sanctions implementation committee from even meeting for much of the first half of 2010 (CRS 2010, 8).

12. In addition, UNSC Resolution 1695 prohibits North Korea's export or import of missiles and missile-related technology, and also bans any financial transactions associated with its nuclear or missile programs. However, China steadfastly blocked UNSC discussion of further sanctions in the wake of the Yeonpyeong shelling. One possible explanation for their reticence to address the issue is that any further sanctions would go after commercial trade, which the Chinese have shown an extreme reluctance to do.

13. UNSC Resolution 1718 imposed an embargo on exports of heavy weapons, dual-use items, and luxury goods to North Korea, as well as a ban on the importation of heavy weapons systems from North Korea. UNSC 1874, passed in the aftermath of the May 2009 test, marginally extended sanctions to include all arms-related trade, as well as all training or assistance related to it (such as suspected cooperation with both Syria and Iran).

14. In 2007, China reported arms and ammunition exports to North Korea of US$20,000, consisting entirely of cartridges for shotguns.

15. These results are consistent with the CRS (2010) finding, based on the US sanctions list, that Chinese exports of luxury goods to North Korea have risen after each UN resolution.

16. An important loophole is that such interdiction must have the consent of the country under which the vessel is flagged; acting under Chapter 7, Article 41,

UNSC Resolution 1874 does not authorize the use of force. If the flag state does not consent, then "the flag state shall direct the vessel to proceed to an appropriate and convenient port for the required inspection." Nonetheless, the resolution does impose constraints because the major flags of convenience, such as Panama and Liberia, will come under strong pressure to comply, while failure to cooperate allows states to deny ships bunkering services. In 2009, a shadowed North Korean ship believed to be headed to Myanmar was ultimately forced to return to North Korea. The resolution also precludes the provision of bunkering services to any ship suspected of prohibited trade. See United Nations Security Council (2010) for further detail.

17. Interestingly, economic activity (GDP) in North Korea had no effect on these items either, suggesting that their provision is driven by politics rather than demand; visual inspection of price-adjusted exports of these items shows a relatively constant level of food and fuel exports over the entire period of the second crisis.

18. The three categories are constructed from data provided by the Ministry of Unification as follows: "Aid" is the sum of government and civilian aid, support for the construction of the light water reactors (LWR) and fuel oil shipments promised under the 1994 Agreed Framework, and energy assistance provided as an inducement for agreements struck through the Six Party Talks in 2007–2008. "Commercial trade" is the sum of general commission trade and the processing on such trade. "Cooperation projects" include trade in conjunction with the Kaesong Industrial Complex, the Kumgang tourist project, and other cooperation projects the government has periodically launched (light industry projects, social and cultural cooperation, etc.)

19. We now have numerous accounts of the progress and lack of progress in the Six Party Talks, but several accounts stand out for the thoroughness of their reporting, including Sigal 2005, Funabashi 2007, Pritchard 2007, Mazarr 2007, Chinoy 2008, and Bechtol 2010.

20. Following the onset of the crisis, the United States clearly had reason to doubt North Korean commitments under the Agreed Framework. But the Agreed Framework also called for a process of normalization of relations with the United States that made limited progress during the Clinton administration.

21. On the eve of Kim Dae-jung's visit to Washington, Powell told reporters that the Bush administration would build on the Clinton momentum on North Korea. The White House publicly rebuked Powell, who later admitted that he had leaned "too forward in my skis." The first statement of a willingness to engage, however vague and hedged, came following the completion of the policy review. See "Statement of the President," June 13, 2001, at http://georgewbush-whitehouse .archives.gov/news/releases/2001/06/20010611-4.html.

22. Remarks at the Asia Society annual dinner, June 10, 2002, at http://asiasociety .org/policy-politics/colin-powell-remarks-asia-society-annual-dinner-2002.

23. Most notable in this regard were the Nuclear Posture Review submitted to Congress in December 2001—to which the North Koreans responded strongly—and the National Strategy to Combat Weapons of Mass Destruction, issued in December 2002.

24. Particularly John Bolton, then undersecretary of state for arms control and international security, "Beyond the Axis of Evil: Additional Threats from Weapons of Mass Destruction," The Heritage Foundation, May 6, 2001, at http://www .heritage.org/Research/Lecture/Beyond-the-Axis-of-Evil. Also, "North Korea: A Shared Challenge to the U.S. and ROK," Korean-American Association, Seoul, August 29, 2002.

25. "Spokesman of DPRK Foreign Ministry on Bush's Statement on Resuming Negotiations with DPRK," June 21, 2001, and "KCNA on U.S.-Proposed Resumption of DPRK-U.S. Negotiations," June 28, 2001, at http://www.kcna.co.jp/index-e.htm.

26. Frank Januzzi (2003) reports a North Korean version of the Kelly visit, and Pyongyang's expectation of an offer to negotiate. See also Doug Struck, "North Korean Program Not Negotiable, U.S. Told N. Korea," *Washington Post*, October 20, 2002, A-18.

27. For the debate over the extent of the program, see Hersh 2003, the exchange between Harrison 2005 and Reiss and Galucci 2005, Pinkston 2007, Zhang 2009, and NTI 2010. In Pervez Musharraf's memoir (2006, 296), he states that a 1996 deal included "nearly two dozen P-1 and P-2 centrifuges," specialized equipment such as a flow meter and oils, and training at Pakistani facilities. Other intelligence in the public domain includes purchases of equipment, including aluminum tubes, that could have been used in an HEU program, as well as traces of HEU on documents subsequently submitted to the United States in 2008 (Zhang 2009).

28. See the Foreign Ministry statement, "Conclusion of Non-aggression Treaty between DPRK and U.S. Called For," KCNA, October 25, 2002, at http://www.kcna .co.jp/index-e.htm.

29. This set of measures came to be called the Illicit Activities Initiative. See Asher 2007 for a brief overview of the program.

30. The release of Rumsfeld's 2011 memoir was accompanied by the launch of a website—the Rumsfeld Papers at http://www.rumsfeld.com/—with a searchable database of documents.

31. Donald Rumsfeld to Richard Cheney, Colin Powell, George Tenet, Spencer Abraham, and Condoleezza Rice, "Remaining Firm on North Korea," December 26, 2002.

32. Again, the Rumsfeld papers provide interesting insight. In a memo with wide distribution among the top leadership, including the vice president and the secretaries of defense, state, treasury, and energy, as well as the chairman of the joint chiefs, National Security Council Advisor Condoleezza Rice outlines a broad strategy for dealing with North Korea, on which Rumsfeld comments. Her draft says, "We have proposed multilateral talks to North Korea and remain prepared to engage in such talks. In this multilateral format, we are prepared to discuss all issues, including DPRK interest in security assurances." Rumsfeld responds by striking out the second sentence. Even internally, inducements are couched in vague terms, and only following complete compliance with its obligations: "Should North Korea verifiably eliminate its nuclear weapons program...it will find that the international community, including the United States, is prepared to respond." Condoleezza Rice to Vice President Richard Cheney et al., "North Korea Policy Points," March 4, 2003.

33. Ser Myo-ja, "North Korea Details Its Plan to End Crisis," *Joongang Daily*, August 28, 2003, at http://joongangdaily.joins.com/article/view.asp?aid=2025739.

34. The following draws on the excellent account of Kim 2009.

35. The shipments of 1 million metric tons (MT) of heavy fuel oil or equivalent were to be divided equally by the five parties: 200,000 MT each. Over the next fourteen months, HFO shipments were slowed in part by disagreements among the parties and in part by logistical issues; see Appendix 3 for information on the delivery of HFO by the five parties and the timing of oil shipments. By March 2009, North Korea had received 500,000 MT of heavy fuel oil and equipment and 245,110 MT of fuel equivalent assistance (Manyin and Nikitin 2010).

36. A sense of the intense political pressure on the administration's policy and a clear statement of the use of verification to address it can be found in Condoleezza Rice's "Remarks at Heritage Foundation on U.S. Policy in Asia," June 18, 2008, at http://www.america.gov/st/texttrans-english/2008/June/20080619140227eaifas0.8862574.html.

37. "Foreign Ministry's Spokesman on DPRK's Decision to Suspend Activities to Disable Nuclear Facilities," August 26, 2008, at http://www.kcna.co.jp/index-e.htm.

38. The new agreement, of which critical components were transmitted only in verbal form, allowed "sampling and other forensic measures" at the three declared sites at Yongbyon--the reactor, reprocessing plant, and fuel fabrication plant—and access to undeclared sites, but only on mutual consent.

39. Rumsfeld to Bush, "Declaratory Policy and the Nuclear Programs of North Korea and Iran," October 5, 2006, at http://www.rumsfeld.com/.

40. North Korea contests the legal status of the islands, arguing that both the drawing of the Northern Limit Line and the inclusion of the islands to the south of it were unilateral actions by the UN Command. See International Crisis Group 2011.

41. Sigal (2009) notes open references by Secretary of State Clinton to the succession, labeling North Korea a "tyranny," and appointing a special envoy—Stephen Bosworth—who concurrently held a full-time position outside government.

42. See Stephen Bosworth, special representative for North Korea policy, remarks at the Korea Society annual dinner, Washington, DC, June 9, 2009; Secretary Clinton's statement for her confirmation hearings on January 13 at http://www.state.gov/secretary/rm/2009a/01/115196.htm; and Clinton's interview with Yoichi Funabashi and Yoichi Kato of *Asahi Shimbun*, Tokyo, Japan, February 17, 2009, at http://www.state.gov/secretary/rm/2009a/02/117626.htm.

43. "DPRK Foreign Ministry's Spokesman Dismisses U.S. Wrong Assertion," January 13, 2009, and, as amended following Hillary Clinton's nomination hearings on January 17, 2009, at http://www.kcna.co.jp/index-e.htm. North Korea's commitment to denuclearization was signaled only very indirectly through Chinese sources following the visit of Wang Jiarui, chief of the International Liaison Department of the Chinese Communist Party (CCP), to Pyongyang in January 2009. See Xinhua, "Top DPRK Leader Kim Jong Il Meets with Visiting CPA Official," January 23, 2008, at http://news.xinhuanet.com/english/2009-01/23/content_10707546.htm.

44. Paragraph 2 "demands that the DPRK not conduct any further nuclear test or launch of a ballistic missile."

45. "DPRK Foreign Ministry Vigorously Refutes UNSC's 'Presidential Statement,'" April 14, 2009, at http://www.kcna.co.jp/index-e.htm.

46. For an overview of China's bilateral response to the test, see Kenji Minemura, "N. Korea Squirms after China Raps Test," *Asahi Shimbun*, February 24, 2010, at http://www.asahi.com/english/TKY201002230434.html.

47. See UNSC (2010) for further details.

48. In addition to three North Korean companies, the United States also targeted Hong Kong Electronics, a firm suspected of funneling money from Iran that was used in North Korea's nuclear program. On the financial sanctions, see Financial Crimes Enforcement Network Advisory, "North Korean Government Agencies and Front Companies Involvement in Illicit Financial Activities," June 18, 2009, at http://www.fincen.gov/statutes_regs/guidance/html/fin-2009-a002.html.

49. The first report of this panel (UNSC 2010) was released in November 2010, reportedly after months of delay due to Chinese objections (Congressional Research Service 2010).

50. An announcement was issued in November that the task of weaponizing extracted plutonium had been completed. With respect to enrichment, a September letter to the president of the UN Security Council, once again denouncing the sanctions, noted cryptically that "experimental uranium enrichment has successfully been conducted to enter into completion phase."

51. With respect to the United States, former President Clinton was allowed to visit Pyongyang in August 2009 to secure the release of two detained journalists. That month also saw a more extensive set of initiatives in North-South relations, including an agreement between North Korea and the Hyundai Group to resume cross-border tourism, ease border controls, and facilitate cross-border family reunions, as well as facilitate direct talks with a delegation in South Korea for Kim Dae-jung's funeral.

52. For example, when Ambassador Bosworth went to Pyongyang in December 2009 for "discussions," the United States was insistent that these had taken place "within the framework" of the Six Party Talks.

53. See Assistant Secretary of State Kurt M. Campbell, "Press Availability in Beijing, China," October 14, 2009, at http://www.state.gov/p/eap/rls/rm/2009/10/130578.htm.

54. "DPRK Proposes to Start of Peace Talks," KCNA, January 11, 2010, at http://www.kcna.co.jp/index-e.htm.

55. A variety of other formulations about venue are visible over the course of 2009–2010, with statements making reference to the Six Party Talks often coming in the wake of meetings with the Chinese. Nonetheless, these statements are laced with ambiguity about the country's intentions. After a meeting with the Chinese leadership in October 2009, Kim Jong-il stated, "We expressed our readiness to hold multilateral talks, depending on the outcome of the DPRK-US talks. The Six Party Talks are also included in the multilateral talks." This suggests both the importance of bilateral talks and the fact that multilateral talks must not be limited to

the Six Party Talks ("Kim Jong Il Visits Wen Jiabao at State Guest House," KCNA, October 5, 2009). A July statement says that "the DPRK will make consistent efforts for the conclusion of a peace treaty and the denuclearization through the Six Party Talks conducted on equal footing." ("Foreign Ministry on UN Presidential Statement on 'Cheonan,'" KCNA, July 10, 2010.)

56. Although the Lee administration chose to protect the Kaesong and Kumgang projects, both were ultimately affected by the changed environment.

57. The Northern Limit Line (NLL) was drawn unilaterally by the United Nations Command following a failure to agree on a maritime border during the armistice negotiations. The NLL had effectively served as the de facto maritime boundary in the Yellow Sea for decades, but North Korea began to contest it in the 1970s for a combination of strategic and economic reasons. Armed clashes occurred around the NLL in 1999, 2002, and 2004.

58. Similar patterns of escalation were visible around the Kaesong and Kumgang projects.

59. The presidential statement of July 9 did not explicitly identify the North Koreans as the perpetrators and took note of their objection that they had nothing to do with the event. But the Chinese acceptance of language identifying the sinking as an "attack" was quickly interpreted by the United States as an admission of North Korea's culpability (Lynch 2010). However, within the UNSC, China continued to protect North Korea by seeking to avoid any linkage between the sinking of the *Cheonan* and existing or further sanctions (CRS 2010).

60. Among the North Korean entities designated under the new sanctions were the Reconnaissance General Bureau, a newly formed intelligence organization also involved in conventional arms trade and suspected of involvement in the *Cheonan* incident; its commander, Lt. Gen. Kim Yong-chol; Green Pine Associated Corp., a front company controlled by the Reconnaissance General Bureau and involved in the arms trade; and the notorious "Office 39" of the Workers' Party of Korea, long believed to provide slush funds to the top leadership, including through receipts from illicit activities. See UNSC (2010) for further details.

61. The International Criminal Court (ICC) stepped into the vacuum created by UNSC inaction, with prosecutor Luis Moreno-Ocampo announcing on December 6 that he was opening a war investigation into both the sinking of the *Cheonan* and the shelling of Yeonpyeong Island that occurred in the territory of South Korea, an ICC signatory. Moreno-Ocampo indicated that the investigation was being launched in response to entreaties from South Korean citizens, not by an official request, though some observers believed that the South Korean government probably requested the investigation. The United States is not an ICC signatory and does not have standing in the court (John Pomfret, "International Criminal Court Probes Alleged North Korean War Crimes," *Washington Post*, December 6, 2010; Edith M. Lederer, "International Court Investigating North Korea," Associated Press, December 7, 2010).

62. Interestingly, Siegfried Hecker held this view.

63. See, for example, the comments of Assistant Secretary of State Kurt M. Campbell before the Senate Foreign Relations Committee: http://foreign.senate.gov/hearings/hearing/?id=e85bfd8f-5056-a032-528b-0969fbfd6ecc.

64. Once such investigations are initiated, they cannot be terminated diplomatically. See http://www.thepeninsulaqatar.com/middle-east/144513-icc-targets-gaddafi-3 -sons-and-4-aides.html.

65. "Rice in the husk or not, not further prepared."

66. According to COMTRADE, Japan exported 500,000 metric tons of rice valued at US$1,017 million in 2001. This implies that the reported price of Japanese rice exports for this year was $2,034/MT, over 10 times the 12-month average price of 5 percent broken milled white rice of $173/MT for 2001 reported in the IMF Primary Commodity Prices database. Interestingly, if we subtract out the $1,017 million of rice imports from the $1,169 million of total imports from Japan for 2001 as reported in DOTS, reprice the rice exports based on the average price of milled white rice for 2001, adjust by a factor of 1.1 for cif, and add this number to the difference between the IMF's total North Korean imports from Japan and COMTRADE's Japanese rice exports to North Korea, the value of North Korea's total imports from Japan would be approximately $247 million for 2001, almost equal to the $249 million reported by KOTRA. It should be noted that this exercise is merely for illustrative purposes, and that ultimately it is impossible to tell whether the source of the enormous discrepancy discussed above comes from an exercise such as this, a stripping out of "aid," or some other factor.

67. Currently we have bilateral trade from DOTS for all years in this study (1990–2005), but only have a bilateral breakdown of trade data from KOTRA for years 2001–2004.

68. For a full description of the Harmonized System, see http://unstats.un.org/unsd /tradekb/Knowledgebase/Harmonized-Commodity-Description-and-Coding-Systems-HS

Bibliography

Asher, David L. 2007. "The Impact of U.S. Policy on North Korean Illicit Activities." *Heritage Lectures* 1024. Washington, DC: Heritage Foundation, May 23.

Bechtol, Bruce. 2010. *Defiant Failed State: The North Korean Threat to International Security.* Washington, DC: Potomac Books.

Bolton, John. 2007. *Surrender Is Not an Option: Defending America at the United Nations.* New York: Threshold Editions.

Brooks, Risa A. 2002. "Sanctions and Regime Type: What Works, and When?" *Security Studies* 11(4): 1–50.

Carlin, Robert L., and Joel Wit. 2006. "North Korean Reform: Politics, Economics, Security." Adelphi Working Paper No. 382. London: International Institute for Strategic Studies.

Chinoy, Michael. 2008. *Meltdown: The Inside Story of the North Korean Nuclear Crisis.* New York: St. Martin's Press.

Choi, Jinwook. 2009. "Why Is North Korea So Aggressive? Kim Jong-il's Illness and North Korea's Changing Governing Style." Nautilus Institute Policy Forum Online 09-062A, July 30. http://www.nautilus.org/publications/essays/napsnet/forum/2009-2010/09062Choi.html/.

Congressional Research Service (CRS). 2010. "Implementation of U.N. Security Council Resolution 1874," October 8, http://lugar.senate.gov/issues/foreign/ (accessed November 6, 2010).

Cortright, David, and George A. Lopez, eds. 2002. *Smart Sanctions: Targeted Economic Statecraft.* New York: Rowman and Littlefield.

Drezner, Daniel. 1999–2000. "The Trouble with Carrots: Transaction Costs, Conflict Expectations, and Economic Inducements." *Security Studies* 9(1/2): 188–218.

Eberstadt, Nicholas. 2004. "The Persistence of North Korea." *Policy Review* 127, October/November 2004, http://www.hoover.org/publications/policy-review/article/6592.

———. 2009. "What Went Wrong? The Bush Administration's Failed North Korea Policy," *The Weekly Standard* 14, January 26.

Elliott, Kimberly Ann. 2010. "Responding to North Korean Provocations: Limitations of Sanctions." *International Journal of Korean Unification Studies*, forthcoming.

Frank, Ruediger. 2005. "Economic Reforms in North Korea (1998–2004): Systemic Restrictions, Quantitative Analysis, Ideological Background." *Journal of the Asia Pacific Economy* 10(3): 278–311.

Funabashi, Yoichi. 2007. *The Peninsula Question: A Chronicle of the Second North Korean Nuclear Crisis*. Washington, DC: Brookings Institution.

Goodkind, Daniel, and Lorraine West. 2001. "The North Korean Famine and Its Demographic Impact." *Population and Development Review* 27 (2): 219–38.

Haggard, Stephan, and Marcus Noland. 2007. *Famine in North Korea: Markets, Aid, and Reform*. New York: Columbia University Press.

———. 2008. "North Korea's Foreign Economic Relations." *International Relations of the Asia-Pacific* 8(2): 219–46.

———. 2010a. "The Winter of Their Discontent: Pyongyang Attacks the Market." *Policy Brief* 10-1. Washington, DC: Peterson Institute for International Economics.

———. 2010b. "Sanctioning North Korea: The Political Economy of Denuclearization and Proliferation." *Asia Survey* 50(3): 539–68.

———. 2011. "Economic Crime and Punishment in North Korea," *Political Science Quarterly*, forthcoming.

Haggard, Stephan, and Daniel Pinkston. 2010. "Guarding the Guardians: North Korea's Political Institutions in Comparative Perspective." Paper prepared for the Conference on Authoritarianism in East Asia, City University of Hong Kong, June 29–July 1, 2010.

Hall, Kevin. 2008. "U.S. Counterfeiting Charges Against N. Korea Based on Shaky Evidence," *McClatchy*, January 10, http://www.mcclatchydc.com/2008 /01/10/24521/us-counterfeiting-charges-against.html.

Harrison, Selig. 2005. "Did North Korea Cheat?" *Foreign Affairs*, January/February.

Hathaway, Robert M., and Jordan Tama. 2004. "The U.S. Congress and North Korea during the Clinton Years: Talk Tough, Carry a Small Stick." *Asian Survey* 44(5): 711–33.

Hersh, Seymour. 2003. "The Cold Test," *The New Yorker*, January 27.

Hufbauer, Gary Clyde, Jeffrey J. Schott, and Kimberly Ann Elliott. 2009. *Economic Sanctions Reconsidered: History and Current Policy*, 3rd ed. Washington, DC: Institute for International Economics.

Institute for Far Eastern Studies. 2010a. "DPRK Strengthens Control Mechanisms with Revised Law on the People's Economy." *NK Brief* 10-11-26-1. Seoul: Institute for Far Eastern Studies, November, 26.

———. 2010b. "DPRK Restricts Private Car Use, Rattles Markets." *NK Brief* 10-11-01-1. Seoul: Institute for Far Eastern Studies, November 1.

International Crisis Group. 2006. *China and North Korea: Comrades Forever?* Asia Report. 112, February 1, http://www.crisisgroup.org/en/regions/asia/north-east-asia/north-korea/112-china-and-north-korea-comrades-forever.aspx.

———. 2009. *Shades of Red: China's Debate over North Korea.* Asia Report 179, November 2, http://www.crisisgroup.org/en/regions/asia/north-east-asia/north-korea/179-shades-of-red-chinas-debate-over-north-korea.aspx.

———. 2011. *China and Inter-Korean Clashes in the Yellow Sea.* Asia Report 200, January 27, http://www.crisisgroup.org/en/regions/asia/north-east-asia/north-korea/200-china-and-inter-korean-clashes-in-the-yellow-sea.aspx.

Januzzi, Frank S. 2003. "North Korea: Back to the Brink?" in Robert M. Hathaway and Wilson Lee, eds. *George W. Bush and Asia: A Midterm Assessment.* Washington DC: Woodrow Wilson International Center for Scholars.

Jentleson, Bruce W., and Christopher A. Whytock. 2005–2006. "Who 'Won' Libya? The Force-Diplomacy Debate and Its Implications for Theory and Policy." *International Security* 30(3): 47–86.

Kahler, Miles, and Scott Kastner. 2006. "Strategic Uses of Economic Interdependence: Engagement Policies on the Korean Peninsula and across the Taiwan Strait." *Journal of Peace Research* 43(5): 523–41.

Kim, Shin Yong. 2009. "The Torturous Dilemma: The 2008 Six-Party Talks and U.S.-DPRK Relations." In *SAIS U.S.-Korea Yearbook 2008.* Washington, DC: Johns Hopkins University.

Kim, Yeon Geon. 2006. "Japanese Luxury Goods Sanctions on North Korea and Its Estimates." KOTRA Report: Northeast Asia (December) [in Korean], at http://www.globalwindow.org (accessed on December 5, 2008).

Koh, B.C. 2004. "Six-Party Talks: Round Three." Nautilus Institute Policy Forum Online 04-26, July 1, http://oldsite.nautilus.org/fora/security/0426A_Koh.html.

———. 2005. "'Military-First Politics' and Building a 'Powerful and Prosperous Nation' in North Korea." Nautilus Institute Policy Forum Online 05-32A, http://www.relooney.info/SI_FAO-Asia/N-Korea_157.pdf.

Korea Trade-Investment Promotion Agency (KOTRA). 2006. "Details and Trade Amounts of Japan's Luxury Goods Export Sanctions against DPRK." [In Korean.]

Korean Central News Agency (KCNA). 2010. "Joint New Year Editorial," January 1, http://www.kcna.co.jp/index-e.htm (available under "Past News").

Lee, Suk. 2003. "Food Shortages and Economic Institutions in the Democratic People's Republic of Korea." PhD dissertation, University of Warwick, Coventry, United Kingdom.

Lim, Jae-cheon. 2009. *Kim Jong Il's Leadership of North Korea.* New York: Routledge.

Lynch, Colum. 2010. "You Think the Cheonan Statement Was Weak? It Could Have Been Worse," *Foreign Policy,* July 9, http://turtlebay.foreignpolicy.com/posts/2010/07/09/you_think_the_cheonan_statement_was_weak_it_could_have_been_worse.

Manyin, Mark E., and Mary Beth Nikitin. 2010. *Foreign Assistance to North Korea.* Report R40095. Washington, DC: Congressional Research Service of the Library of Congress, March 12.

Mazarr, Michael J. 2007. "The Long Road to Pyongyang: A Case Study in Policymaking Without Direction," *Foreign Affairs* September–October.

McEachern, Patrick. 2008. "Interest Groups in North Korean Politics." *Journal of East Asian Studies* 8(3): 235–58.

McGlynn, John. 2007a. "North Korean Criminality Examined: The US Case, Part 1," *The Asia-Pacific Journal: Japan Focus,* http://www.japanfocus.org/-John-McGlynn /2423.

———. 2007b. "Financial Sanctions and North Korea: In Search of the Evidence of Currency Counterfeiting and Money Laundering, Part 2," *The Asia-Pacific Journal: Japan Focus,* http://www.japanfocus.org/-John-McGlynn/2463

———. 2007c. "Banco Delta Asia, North Korea's Frozen Funds and US Undermining of the Six-Party Talks: Obstacles to a Solution, Part 3," *The Asia-Pacific Journal: Japan Focus,* http://www.japanfocus.org/-John-McGlynn/2446.

Milner, Helen, and Keiko Kubota. 2005. "Why the Move to Free Trade? Democracy and Trade Policy in the Developing Countries." *International Organization* 59: 107–43.

Musharraf, Pervez. 2006. *In the Line of Fire.* New York: Free Press.

National Committee on North Korea. 2007. "In the News: North Korea and Banco Delta Asia," June 26.

Nincic, Miroslav. 2005. *Renegade Regimes: Confronting Deviant Behavior in World Politics.* New York: Columbia University Press.

Noland, Marcus. 2000. *Avoiding the Apocalypse: The Future of the Two Koreas.* Washington, DC: Institute for International Economics.

———. 2004. "The Political Economy of North Korea: Historical Background and Present Situation." In Ahn, Choong-young, Nicholas Eberstadt, and Young-sun Lee eds. 2004. *A New International Engagement Framework for North Korea?* Washington, DC: Korea Economic Institute of America.

———. 2009a. "Telecoms in North Korea: Has Orascom Made the Connection?" *North Korea Review,* Spring.

———. 2009b. "The (Non) Impact of UN Sanctions on North Korea." *Asia Policy* 7: 61–88.

Nuclear Threat Initiative (NTI). 2010. "North Korea Profile: Highly Enriched Uranium Capabilities," http://www.nti.org/e_research/profiles/NK/Nuclear/capabilities.html#heu.

Pape, Robert A. 1997. "Why Economic Sanctions Do Not Work." *International Security* 22(2): 90–136.

Pinkston, Daniel. 2007. "Six Parties Adopt Steps for North Korean Denuclearization but Uraniam Enrichment Remains a Major Obstacle," *WMD Insights,* http://cns.miis.edu/other/wmdi070403c.htm.

Pritchard, Charles L. 2007. *Failed Diplomacy: How North Korea Got the Bomb.* Washington, DC: Brookings Institution.

Reiss, Mitchell, and Robert Galucci. 2005. "Red Handed," *Foreign Affairs*, March/April.

Rennack, Dianne E. 2010. *North Korea: Legislative Basis for U.S. Economic Sanctions.* Report R41438. Washington, DC: Congressional Research Service of the Library of Congress, September 29.

Rumsfeld, Donald. 2011. *Known and Unknown: A Memoir.* New York: Sentinel Press.

Sigal, Leon V. 1998. *Disarming Strangers: Nuclear Diplomacy with North Korea.* Princeton: Princeton University Press.

———. 2002. "North Korea Is No Iraq: Pyongyang's Negotiating Strategy," *Arms Control Today*, December.

———. 2005. "Misplaying North Korea and Losing Friends and Influence in Northeast Asia," *The North Korean Nuclear Crisis: Regional Perspectives*, July 12, http://northkorea.ssrc.org/Sigal/.

———. 2009. "Punishing North Korea Won't Work," *Bulletin of the Atomic Scientists*, May 28.

———. 2010. "Looking for Leverage in All the Wrong Places," *38 North*, U.S.-Korea Institute at SAIS, Johns Hopkins University, May 1, www.38north.org/?p=545.

Snyder, Scott. 2009. *China's Rise and the Two Koreas: Politics, Economics, Security.* Boulder: Lynne Rienner Publishers.

Solingen, Etel. 1994. "The Political Economy of Nuclear Restraint." *International Security* 19(2).

———. 2007. *Nuclear Logics: Contrasting Paths in East Asia and the Middle East.* Princeton: Princeton University Press.

Toloraya, Georgy. 2008. "The Six Party Talks: A Russian Perspective," *Asian Perspective*, 32, 4: 45-69.

United Nations Security Council. 2010. *Report of the Panel of Experts Established Pursuant to Resolution 1874 (2009).* New York: United Nations Security Council.

Yonhap News Agency. 2003. *North Korea Handbook.* Seoul: Yonhap News Agency.

Zhang, Hui. 2009. "Assessing North Korea's Uranium Enrichment Capabilities," *Bulletin of the Atomic Scientists*, June 18, http://www.thebulletin.org/web-edition/features/assessing-north-koreas-uranium-enrichment-capabilities.

Acknowledgments

This monograph is an expanded version of a paper first presented at the workshop on Positive and Negative Inducements, Woodrow Wilson International Center for Scholars, Washington, DC, September 1, 2010, and the annual meeting of the American Political Science Association, Washington, DC, September 1–5, 2010. We would like to thank Etel Solingen and the participants in that workshop and John Delury, Gary Hufbauer, Lee Sigal, Steve Sin, Etel Solingen, Scott Snyder, and Wonho Yeon, who made helpful comments on an earlier draft. Jihyeon Jeong and Jennifer Lee provided research assistance. The Smith Richardson and MacArthur Foundations provided financial support.

Policy Studies series
A publication of the East-West Center

Series Editors: Edward Aspinall and Dieter Ernst

Description
Policy Studies provides policy-relevant scholarly analysis of key contemporary domestic and international issues affecting Asia. The editors invite contributions on Asia's economics, politics, security, and international relations.

Notes to Contributors
Submissions may take the form of a proposal or complete manuscript. For more information on the Policy Studies series, please contact the Series Editors.

Editors, *Policy Studies*
East-West Center
1601 East-West Road
Honolulu, Hawai'i 96848-1601
Tel: 808.944.7197
Publications@EastWestCenter.org
EastWestCenter.org/policystudies

www.ingramcontent.com/pod-product-compliance
Lightning Source LLC
Chambersburg PA
CBHW050539280326
41933CB00011B/1645